# Watching and Waiting

Kenneth Stevenson is the Bishop of Portsmouth.

A leading Anglican scholar specializing in liturgy and the history of theology, he is the author of a number of books, including *Do This: The Shape, Style and Meaning of the Eucharist* and *The Lord's Prayer: A Text in Tradition*, both published by SCM-Canterbury Press. With Rowan Williams and Geoffrey Rowell he compiled *Love's Redeeming Work*, a bestselling anthology of Anglican spiritual writing (Oxford University Press).

# Watching and Waiting

*A Guide to the Celebration of Advent*

Kenneth W. Stevenson

CANTERBURY
PRESS

Norwich

First published in 2007 by the Canterbury Press, Norwich
(a publishing imprint of Hymns Ancient & Modern Limited,
a registered charity)
13–17 Long Lane, London EC1A 9PN

www.scm-canterburypress.co.uk

British Library Cataloguing in Publication data

A catalogue record for this book is available
from the British Library

ISBN 978-1-85311-834-0

Typeset by Regent Typesetting
Printed and bound in Great Britain by
William Clowes Ltd, Beccles, Suffolk

# Contents

# Preface

Advent is a strange season. It is frequently ignored or skimmed over, in the rush to get to Christmas. But its main purpose is to make us think about and celebrate God the Coming One, whether he comes in daily discipleship, the annual celebration of the Nativity, or at the end of all things. And we are enabled to do so with the poetic language that the Scriptures, hymns and prayers can bring. It is an open-ended time of watching and waiting.

This little book is largely occasioned by the arrival of *Common Worship: Times and Seasons* (2006). I have been spurred on to write it by these new liturgical provisions and by the absence so far of much about this season that looks at the great Advent truths, the Scripture readings, and the way these confront how we live, especially at this time of year.

In order to give the book an overall coherence, each chapter is based on one of the seven 'O' Antiphons that have accompanied the Magnificat in the final days before Christmas for centuries – starting with 'O Wisdom' and ending with 'O Emmanuel', the inspiration behind one of Advent's loveliest hymns. These antiphons have been revived in Anglican liturgy in more recent times. We shall look at each in turn, chapter by chapter, from the point of view of their overall shape, their biblical sources and imagery and the way these have been interpreted across the centuries, alongside some of the new liturgical material – and all in the wider context of some of today's questions about faith and life. I hope such an approach may prove useful, nourishing, and challenging. It has been tried before with other parts of the Church Year. The underlying message is that if Advent is a summary of the gospel, then these antiphons are a summary of Advent.

Many people, including my colleague, David Brindley, deserve my thanks for the ideas that lie behind the pages that follow in exploring the riddle of Advent. In particular, I should like to thank Sarah and our family for caring for me and praying for me through my present illness: to them this book is dedicated with much love.

Kenneth Stevenson                                    Candlemas, 2007
Bishopsgrove
Fareham

# Introduction:
# Setting the Scene

In the great Cathedral of Århus, brick-built like many of Denmark's medieval churches, is a large painted screen or reredos behind the high altar. Created by the artist Bernt Notke and completed in 1479, it consists of a rich array of panels that can be moved into different positions for the different periods of the Church Year. The festal array, which also doubles up for ordinary time, has St Anne, according to legend the mother of the Virgin Mary, in the centre; St Clement of Rome, to whom the cathedral is dedicated, on her right, and John the Baptist on her left; and they are surrounded by the twelve apostles and other saints. Then there are the Lenten panels, with their poignant portrayals of the events surrounding the passion. The third set, somewhat unexpectedly, focuses primarily on Advent.

That may surprise us. Why should anyone bother with Advent? Surely it is more of a prelude than a liturgical entity of its own? After all, isn't it really only about preparing (vaguely) for the Coming of Christ? Bernt Notke might well have used his energy more effectively by making a set of panels on something else, like the public ministry of Jesus, his teaching and miracles. But he did no such thing – and wisely so. The Advent panels provide us with a bold representation of John the Baptist, holding the Lamb of God (John 1.29) in his left hand, and pointing to him with his right hand. Then over on the right are two episodes from the life of John the Baptist, the baptism of Jesus (Matt. 3.13–17), and his beheading (Matt. 14.1–12).

1

Other panels are of a domestic character. One depicts the martyrdom of St Clement; by tradition he was martyred by being attached to an anchor – hence the appearance of anchors at various points inside the cathedral and outside on the tower. Another depicts Jens Iversen Lange, the fifteenth-century Bishop of Århus responsible for building the chancel and for installing this magnificent reredos. It is as if Advent, with all its fragility, its message of provisionality, were being applied to these two personalities, a first-century Bishop of Rome who gave his life for the faith, and a late medieval Danish Bishop who gave his energies to completing one of the largest cathedrals in Scandinavia.

Those Advent panels, with their mixture of the 'pure' Advent message of John the Baptist, and the more 'composite' message of subsequent followers of Christ, Clement and Lange, beckon us from our everyday lives and stretch us into the less than ordinary terrain of Christian exploration. Advent can't just be about past events, historic Christian certainties, or vague Christian hopes. Advent coaxes us, makes us look to truths and personalities that are beyond our control, that cannot be tamed, whether it is the truth of the Second Advent, that 'he will come in glory to judge the living and the dead', or the Christ who comes to us anew each Christmas. We do the whole truth of Christianity a profound injustice if we banish that Second Advent to a form of life totally unrelated to what we are doing now, or if we crave a sentimental Jesus in a cosy crib, far removed from the discomforts of the stable and odours of domestic livestock, a singularly inconvenient and marginalized arrival-point on this planet for the Saviour of the world. As Rowan Williams has remarked in a sermon, 'Advent is about the essential ambiguity of our religiousness. We live, as human beings, with an enormous hunger to be spoken to, to be touched, to be judged and loved and absolved.'[1]

As is so often the case, art beckons us through our imaginations to what we would otherwise miss. A late medieval gilded screen that provides the focal point for the far end of a great cathedral, which is visited by thousands of people every year, provides a different kind of context for religious – and human – exploration. There is no sense of accumulating an agreed amount of facts and data in order to have 'done' the Århus reredos! Instead, the slow walk up the nave, ascending the few steps into the 'high choir' (as Danes call the chancel), leads the onlooker, whatever be their state of faith, towards a feast of painted figures that can be quite dazzling. The Advent panelling, even though more restrained in its colouring than the festal–ordinary time arrangement, still invites some kind of response. Are we prepared to take in the gaunt, unkempt figure of John the Baptist, at one moment holding Jesus as the Lamb of God, sacrifice and all; at another moment baptizing Jesus, thereby letting him transform his own trademark symbolic action that brought folk out to hear him in the wilderness; and at yet another moment paying the ultimate cost of standing up to paranoid leadership, beheaded by an insecure and threatened local king?

John the Baptist is indeed the gateway to Jesus. But the story of Advent is richer still, and here history can come to our aid. There is a dual tension to the season that had built up over the centuries, a joyous anticipation of the Second Advent, and a (sometimes penitential) preparation for the Coming of Christ at Christmas. Some of the oldest Advent hymns – such as the seventh-century 'Creator alme siderum', 'Creator of the starry height' – retain that earlier focus on joyfully looking forward to the Second Coming.[2] The penitential strand seems to have begun in France, as a fast to prepare for Christmas: that is all, for that matter, that we can find of anything like Advent in the East, where the season itself is unknown, though there is a week of preparation for Christmas. As early as 480 at Tours it was the custom for the monks to fast three times a week, from the feast of St Martin of Tours, 11 November onwards.[3] This increases in rigour in 529, when the monks are required to fast every day in December. Pope Leo the Great in one of his pre-Christmas sermons refers to a fast in general terms, to build up spiritual discipline. Although these fasts do not appear as exacting as in Lent, there is nonetheless more than an echo of Advent–Christmas corresponding with Lent–Holy Week–Easter.

The liturgical 'mood' of Advent, therefore, does offer something of a mixture. This is reflected in changing practices at Rome, where in 1140 the Pope is supposed to celebrate the Eucharist joyously, with festal vestments, and the 'Gloria in excelsis', whereas 150 years later, in 1290, the joyous background has gone, penitential colours are worn, and the 'Gloria in excelsis' is omitted – a clear imitation of Lent. The famous hymn of judgement, 'Dies Irae' ('Day of Wrath'), dates from the thirteenth century, and may well stand behind the shift of Advent in this penitential direction. We must remember, of course, that this evidence is sporadic, to say the least. We can't lump it all together to form a uniform picture. But we have to admit to a picture of some variety, a variety that extends to the *length* of the season. In parts of France there appear to have been three Sundays of Advent, whereas at Milan there were (and remain to this day) six, which we can date around the seventh century. Elsewhere there were five. Pope Gregory the Great, great organizer that he was, reduced what had been a six-Sunday Advent at Rome to four at the end of the sixth century.[4]

Then along comes the question, when is the year supposed to begin? Imperial Rome began it in January; Byzantium in September, which is when the academic year now begins and, for many people, the rhythm of the new year also starts after the summer break. But service-books and lectionaries began to start with Advent from around the eleventh century, which made its own impact on how the 'Church Year' was understood. This is a far cry from a pre-Christmas fast, or a short 'season' to contemplate the Second Coming. It sets what becomes the 'secular' year against the 'ecclesiastical' in a way that produces yet one more tension in this riddle which is Advent. There are many hymns in the Danish repertoire, including a short hymn

4

written in 1849 by N. F. S. Grundtvig, 'Be welcome, the Lord's year' ('Vær velkommen, Herrens år'), which goes through the liturgical year as far as Pentecost, and which is usually sung on Advent Sunday. And yet, in the same year, Grundtvig wrote another four-verse hymn, with the same opening line, to be sung on New Year's Day, which speaks more generally of the grace of God in the life of the believer in daily growth in faith.[5] It is as if Grundtvig is aware of the need to bridge the gap between what we would nowadays call an 'ecclesiastical' and a 'secular' approach to the coming year.

So far, so varied. The older Advent collects repeatedly use verbs that suggest impatience with things as they are. A notable example is the collect that has been used on the Sunday before Advent in the English Prayer Book, and is a relic of an older five-week Advent. It is now used as a post-communion prayer for that Sunday, now kept as the feast of Christ the King:

> Stir up, O Lord,
> the wills of your faithful people;
> that they, plenteously bringing forth the fruit of good works,
> may by you be plenteously rewarded;
> through Jesus Christ our Lord.[6]

'Stir up Sunday', as it became known, was a kind of signal that a change of gear was about to take place (and it also provided, in folk custom, a reminder to prepare the Christmas pudding). Impatience with things as they are underscores so much of the meaning of Advent. But there is another strand that has surfaced in recent decades, perhaps caused by the commercialization of Christmas alongside the growth in popularity of carol services, which is the tendency to start celebrating Christmas early. I have lived with this much of my life, and have even encountered clergy who frown at congregations through purple stoles because the 'real meaning' of Christmas is apparently destroyed if a single carol is sung before 24 December.

Such fundamentalisms, unfortunately, seldom achieve much – apart from setting sacred and secular more and more against each other, which is the very message the incarnation is not about. The old Advent eucharistic readings were not about preparing for Christmas at all, but were about the Coming Christ, coming in our faith, coming at the end of time (Luke 21.25–33), and the tension between Jesus and John the Baptist (Matt. 11.2–16; John 1.19–28). The changes recently made in the lectionary make two definite shifts, apart from a three-year provision that opens up far more Scripture in worship. One is to turn the fourth Sunday of Advent into an unambiguous preparation for the birth of Jesus (Year A has Matt. 1.18–25, the birth narrative, B has Luke 1.26–38, the annunciation, C has Luke 1.39–45, the visitation): this echoes long-established practice at Milan, and has the effect of softening what some take to be a hard divide between Advent and Christmas. The other is to make more of Jesus' teaching about the signs of the Coming Kingdom in the four Sundays before Advent, even naming the Sunday immediately before as 'Christ the King'. The 'Kingdom' season is therefore more of a prelude to Advent than a way of rounding off the previous year, and is appropriately treated alongside Advent, as we shall be doing in these pages.

The feast of Christ the King was instituted in the Roman Catholic Church in 1925, at a time when Europe was undergoing acute political instability. It was to be celebrated on the last Sunday of October. After the Second Vatican Council, it was moved to its present position. Other churches have followed suit, especially those that have followed (and adapted) the three-year Sunday eucharistic lectionary that appeared in 1969 after the Council. For Anglicans, this meant losing something of the old 'Stir up Sunday'. It was a small price to pay for the enriching quality of the 'Kingdom' season, which pushes us away from current concerns, and forces us to look at the Kingship of Christ through three contrasting Gospel passages: Year A has Matt. 25.31–46, the Great Assize; Year B has John 18.33–37, Jesus before Pilate; and Year C has Luke 23.33–43, the crucifixion and the penitent thief. There is nothing cosy here and it is no bad thing to hear such passages when the shopping-spree for Christmas is well under way.

There is, however, a small spanner in the works for Anglicans, which concerns the Second Sunday in Advent. The 1662 Prayer Book collect was specially written at the time of the Reformation to expand on the epistle reading (Rom. 15.4–13), about how the Scriptures were written so that we may 'read, mark, learn, and inwardly digest them'. In *Common Worship*, it now appears as the collect for the Last Sunday after Trinity:

> Blessed Lord,
> who caused all holy Scriptures to be written for our
>   learning:
> help us so to hear them,
> to read, mark, learn and inwardly digest them
> that, through patience, and the comfort of your holy word,
> we may embrace and for ever hold fast
>   the hope of everlasting life,
> which you have given us in our Saviour Jesus Christ,
> who is alive and reigns with you,
> in the unity of the Holy Spirit,
> one God, now and for ever.[7]

For a community having the chance to read the Bible in its mother tongue (instead of through the intermediary of Latin, the language of the Church) this was an understandable development; and, in any case, it makes that collect a winner for private devotion on any occasion, especially before looking at the Scriptures. But the overall consequence was that the Second Sunday in Advent tended to be called 'Bible Sunday', often with sermons about the Bible, how it was translated, and how it continues to be translated into new tongues as the Church's mission extends further and further afield. All well and good – but how much does this relate directly to Advent? 'Bible Sunday' has now in effect been moved to the end of the Trinity season, where it is nearer the Lutheran 'Reformation' Sunday, perhaps a more appropriate home for it. The result of this change is, quite simply, to make the Second Sunday more explicitly to do with Advent.

Before we go any further, a summary is perhaps in order.

1  Advent started life as a pre-Christmas fast for the devout, which is what it still is in the Christian East.
2  By the sixth century, in the Latin West, it was becoming a season in its own right, with a strong emphasis on the Second Coming of Christ.
3  Its length varied, from six Sundays in France and Milan, to four at Rome.
4  Its mood also varied; the joyous celebration of old of the Coming of Christ gradually gave way in the middle ages to a more sombre tone, reflected in the colour of vestments.
5  At the Reformation, the season was kept in Anglican and Lutheran traditions, with some adaptation; and it was, of course, retained in the Roman Catholic Church.
6  The use of blue vestments in the later middle ages provided a contrast with the sombre colours, purple or unbleached linen, for Lent.
7  The long-established custom at Milan of treating the Fourth Sunday as a preparation for Christmas has been recently introduced into the three-year lectionary used by many other churches today.
8  The longer Advent at Milan has been one of the inspirations behind the introduction of the four Sundays before Advent, with their emphasis on the Last Things, the signs of the Coming Kingdom, and with the costly nature of Christ's Kingship.

We have been approaching Advent from four perspectives. The first has been based on a work of art, with its own historical background. The next has been the tangled history of the various strands that helped to make Advent what it is today. The third has been through what comes before Advent – particularly in the recent innovation of what is sometimes called the 'Kingdom' season. And the fourth has been the Bible readings chosen for this time of the year. What we have today, in the almost overwhelming lectionary provisions of the three-year scheme, is far from being the total summit of what has gone before, beyond any correction in the future. It may well be that a generation to come will find the need to simplify, just as Gregory the Great resolutely cut down the six-Sunday scheme to the four with which we have been familiar in the West for the past 1500 years. The Liturgical Year, like everything else to do with worship, does not have some kind of canonical status – only the Bible has that authority.

All this suggests that Advent, for all these variations and changes, is rather bigger than one at first suspects. It is not just a case of keeping something going 'at church' while another rather different world rushes around shopping, cooking, and spending too much money perhaps. Advent, so far from being an isolated set of Sundays that takes us through December to the Christmas crib, is much more. It is a summary of the whole gospel – like the reredos in that Danish cathedral. Every time we approach Advent, we are approaching a God who speaks to us from beyond the manageable and the convenient. Advent is a hidden gem that we easily pass by, perhaps because we are too distracted, or because we have tamed it out of any real significance, and become just too familiar with its narrow confines.

These questions inevitably lead us to a deeper set of contradictions, which are about our own attitudes to God and our faith. Is faith primarily about what we sometimes call the 'hereafter', or is it essentially this-worldly? Of course it is about both, held together in tension, which is why Advent is the time of year when we can think about that relationship more profoundly than perhaps at any other time. Surrounded by consumerism on every side, we find it has invaded religious practice, even our sometimes too specific expectations of what the Church should provide us with. There is indeed a religious form of consumerism that may well have landed us with a liturgy sometimes so overloaded with words that it requires thinning down (one of my colleagues once remarked, 'few draft orders of service leave the bishop's study lengthened'). It is therefore all the more important to make a little go a long way, to pause and ponder specific liturgical texts and prayers (as we shall be doing throughout this book), so that the sometimes all too familiar is enabled to reveal hidden riches of which we were never fully aware.

The word *adventus* was used to refer to the solemn arrival of a god, and by extension the emperor, in Ancient Rome. There was something momentous about the word, a far cry from any sense of Advent as a convenience, or an excuse for serving up a particular message to meet a particular spiritual need of the moment. Advent has to sit uncomfortably with the secular world that it inhabits – and quietly judges, as it points us to the coming judgement of things as they are, whether through Bethlehem or at the end of time. Advent would, one suspects, be better served by the slogan 'Make Poverty History' than the relentless pressure from advertisers and retailers to spend and spend. The frenetic commercialism that is the backdrop to Advent, focused on 'getting ready for Christmas', is a comparatively new phenomenon. Giving presents grew out of the custom of imitating the generosity of St Nicholas, whose day falls on 6 December; although there are those who link it with the much older Jewish festival of *Hanukkah*, when gifts are exchanged in the family and the community.

Having 'approached' Advent in this multifaceted way, we have to confront it and consider it in a manner that takes us to those depths that can be so easily avoided. But how shall we do this? One particular liturgical route is provided by the rich series of antiphons on the Coming of God into the world that have normally been used from 17 to 23 December in connection with the Magnificat, the Song of Mary (Luke 1.46–55). The Magnificat, sung at Evening Prayer by Western Christians of many kinds for centuries, is the first of a series of canticles that are unique to Luke's Gospel. The remaining ones are the Song of Zechariah, the Benedictus ('Blessed be the Lord, the God of Israel', Luke 1.68–79), the Song of the Angels, the Gloria in excelsis ('Glory to God in the highest', Luke 2.14), and the Song of Simeon, the Nunc Dimittis ('Now, Lord, you let your servant go in peace', Luke 2.29–32). Each of them, even the Gloria in excelsis in all its brevity (it was soon added to, and became the now familiar hymn at the start of the normal Sunday Eucharist), tells of the gift and the reality of God's redemption. But for our purposes, it is the Magnificat that stands out the most:

> My soul proclaims the greatness of the Lord,
> my spirit rejoices in God my Saviour;
> he has looked with favour on his lowly servant.
>
> From this day all generations will call me blessed;
> the Almighty has done great things for me
> and holy is his name.
>
> He has mercy on those who fear him,
> from generation to generation.
>
> He has shown strength with his arm
> and has scattered the proud in their conceit,
>
> Casting down the mighty from their thrones
> and lifting up the lowly.
>
> He has filled the hungry with good things
> and sent the rich away empty.
>
> He has come to the aid of his servant Israel,
> to remember his promise of mercy,
>
> The promise made to our ancestors,
> to Abraham and his children for ever.[8]

It is worth pausing to take in the intricate structure of this liturgical masterpiece. The opening words praise God for his wonderful works, and it then goes on to enumerate them in three ways. First, God is praised for his regard for Mary's lowliness, for deeming her blessed and for doing great things, the implication being that God will continue to perform wonders through the lowly and bless them. Then God is described in two ways – in the holiness of his name, and as possessed of a mercy that extends to all who fear him. That leads into three further descriptions of the way God deals with his people: showing strength to scatter the proud, and then in terms of two major kinds of reversal – casting down the mighty and lifting up the lowly, and filling the hungry while sending the rich away empty. And all this is founded on the reality of redemption through history summarized in the conclusion – God coming to the aid of Israel here and now, just as he did to Abraham and his descendants of old.[9]

It goes without saying that these truths apply to every single day of the Christian's struggle with faith, and every single season of the Church Year. But they have a strong Advent significance, in the confidence of those opening words with their promise of redemption, and how that redemption is so powerfully described in the ensuing images – especially those reversals, a gospel truth if ever there was one – as well as the conclusion, in the way it looks back to Israel's past and forward to the future. Nor must we forget the original context of the Magnificat – Mary's response to the promise of the birth of the Saviour, and all that this will mean for the whole world. No wonder, therefore, that it is around the Magnificat that these seven antiphons are based, meditations on God's promised redemption. They may well date back to the sixth century, a particularly rich time in the development of the Divine Office in the West. They blossomed into a whole collection of similarly formed compositions: sixteen others like them are known to have been used in Advent.

Antiphons have long been used in order to point up a particular feature of a psalm or canticle. These antiphons, however, are unlike any other, for they are made up of a group of seven, with the same structure – an invocation, followed by a brief description of the context, and concluding with an urgent plea for God to 'come' and save his people.[10] They thus encapsulate the dynamic of 'watching and waiting' which is part of the riddle of Advent. Originally sung at Evening Prayer (Vespers) with the Magnificat, they sometimes migrated to Morning Prayer (Lauds), in order to be sung with the Benedictus. Here are the opening words of each one:

17 December – O Sapientia – O Wisdom
18 December – O Adonai – O Lord
19 December – O Radix Jesse – O Root of Jesse
20 December – O Clavis David – O Key of David
21 December – O Oriens – O Morning Star
22 December – O Rex Gentium – O King of the nations
23 December – O Emmanuel – O God with us

Each antiphon is made up of material mainly from the Old Testament, which we shall be looking at in some detail. The important point to grasp at this stage is the order in which they come.

- God is invoked for his Wisdom, as an opener – Wisdom not as an attribute of God, but as God himself.
- Only then we invoke God as he speaks through the Law, as our Lord: the way some Christians speak and behave today, one would conclude a rush to the Law is the first port of call.
- The Root of Jesse takes us to Israel's – and our own – sacred past, only to confront our need to look critically at what we have inherited: Jesus does not come to affirm all that we are and have been, but to disturb, challenge and encourage us into new paths.
- The image of the Key of David brings us face to face with the issue of access; and in a world of much social exclusion and a great deal of sentimental religious talk about inclusiveness, that is vital.

- Then our souls are lifted from those two images, the past transformed, and the points of access, so that we face the sheer reality of hope, with the Morning Star, ever-rising, and ever-ready to heal.
- But the grandeur of that image then makes us aware of other people, those who share our faith but in a different way, those on the edge of the whole religious enterprise, and those who have a different faith altogether: these Jesus comes to be among as well, as the King of the nations.
- Finally, God is 'with' us as Emmanuel, summing up the previous six invocations, and bringing them into the heart of the 'Coming' of God into our world.

The chapters of this book focus on each of these antiphons in turn and thus they become the basis for further observation and exploration, as we watch and wait through Advent, and as a summary of Advent itself.[11] No specific timeframe is expected. After all, Advent is open-ended and risky: open-ended because of what it seeks to proclaim; and risky because of its inherent uncertainty. Of course each one of us wants to make each one of those antiphons a way of life for ourselves. We all want to be wise, provide spiritual leadership, handle tradition creatively, live and proclaim a God who is accessible, hold on to hope in the darkest times, not behave as if we alone occupy the world's only spiritual space (other people do exist), and do all this as naturally as if God were indeed among us and with us, a true Emmanuel.

Advent both expresses and summarizes the whole gospel, the good news of a Coming One, preparing us for a Kingdom that will always be about unfulfilment – on this earth. That, at the end of the day, is what the Gospels keep telling us. Advent's genius is to help us on this path, and to look for another King, another Kingdom. And one way to do so is through the message of these antiphons, as sacred accompaniments to the song of eternal redemption.

## Notes

1 Rowan Williams, *Open to Judgement: Sermons and Addresses* (London: Darton, Longman & Todd, 1996), p. 7.

2 Patrick Cowley, *Advent: Its Liturgical Significance* (Alcuin Club Tracts) (London: SPCK, 1960), p. 68.

3 Cowley, *Advent*, p. 78.

4 See the discussion of the mass-formulae and lections in Antoine Chavasse, *Le Sacramentaire Gélasien (Vaticanus Reginensis 316): Sacramentaire Presbytéral en usage dans les titres romains au VIIe siècle* (Bibliothèque de Théologie: Série IV: Histoire de la Théologie Vol. I) (Paris: Desclée, 1957), pp. 412–25.

5 *Den Danske Salmebog* (Copenhagen: Det Kgl. Vajsenhus' Forlag, 2003), Nos 74, 712.

6 See *Common Worship: Services and Prayers for the Church of England* (London: Church House Publishing, 2000), p. 426.

7 See *Common Worship: Services and Prayers for the Church of England*, p. 422.

8 See *Common Worship: Services and Prayers for the Church of England*, p. 42.

9 See C. F. Evans, *Saint Luke* (New Testament Commentaries) (London: SCM/Philadelphia: Trinity Press International, 1990), pp. 171ff.; see also Raymond E. Brown, *The Birth of the Messiah* (new updated edition) (London: Chapman, 1993), pp. 355ff.

10 For the texts of the antiphons, see *Common Worship: Times and Seasons* (London: Church House Publishing, 2006), pp. 58–9. The medieval English 'Sarum' rite has eight antiphons, with an additional one ('O Virgin of virgins') in honour of the Virgin Mary, which was not uncommon at the time, and therefore begins these antiphons a day earlier; this explains why in the Prayer Book Calendar the words 'O Sapientia' appear on 16 December.

11 A view taken by Dom Prosper Guéranger, *L'année liturgique: L'Avent Liturgique* (Le Mans: Fleurot, 1841), p. 468; see Sylvain Gasser, 'Les Antiennes "O"', *Etudes Grégoriennes* 24 (1992), p. 53 (whole article, pp. 53–84, a study mainly of the chants used); I am indebted to Harald Buchinger for drawing my attention to this.

# I

# *Wisdom*

## O Sapientia

*O Wisdom, coming forth from the mouth of the Most High,*
*reaching from one end of the earth to the other mightily,*
*and sweetly ordering all things:*
*Come and teach us the way of prudence.*

Information technology has revolutionized our lives. It has
meant that at the press of a button, a document of any size,
whether of a few sentences or of many pages, can be transmit-
ted from one part of the earth to another – and 'mightily',
to echo the Wisdom antiphon. It's not just a case of the capacity to do so. It's the power of these new developments that
can sometimes assault us. I do not think I am alone in being
somewhat ambivalent about all this. On the one hand, I like
to be able to send a friend or colleague something I have written, perhaps for comment or information. On the other hand,
there is more than a tedium in being on the receiving end of
vast amounts of material in which I have very little interest.
Like all advances in any kind of science or technology, it is a
mixed blessing.

To state the obvious in this way is to take a major step from
mere description of the age of the computer to making value-
judgements about the effect this has on people, their lives,
their powers of concentration, their inner souls. I often muse
at what it was like, for example, to write a book 25 years ago
when I had no computer. While the typewriter made me com-

mit myself to a final text in a way that the word-processor no longer does, I can vividly recall using liquid paper in order to make my (all too numerous) corrections, and because I am short-sighted and liquid paper is made of strongly smelling acids, I would inevitably end up with a headache.

But this is all very innocent, and goes little way to grasping the issue, which is the harm that can be done by overloading the human mind with a mountain of data that is supposed – all of it – to be of earth-shattering significance. Meetings seem to require increasing amounts of photocopied paperwork, and yet the gatherings of bishops are invariably improved when the agenda is freed up, and we can really communicate with each other at a deep level about what it is like to be Christian leaders in today's world, teachers of the Catholic faith, messengers of the everlasting gospel. The same observations are made by others in similar positions. 'Don't bother to read too carefully the background papers,' I have often been told. 'It simply clouds the mind!' That could, of course, mean that some official has buried an important change in policy somewhere in the documents in order to be overlooked in the decision-making process. But on the whole, it's safe to say that paperwork is as little read from start to finish as are recipe books for cooking – the difference being that the latter might make more enjoyable reading.

Information technology has obviously brought many blessings, but when misused, it can lead to information overload, even in the simplest way, like listening to too many news programmes. We human beings may be gifted in different ways, with different personalities. Some of us may be good at absorbing information, retaining it and (perhaps most important of all) filtering it for the use of others. But once we speak of the filtering process, we are making another kind of value-judgement, which begs the question that there might be criteria for extracting what 'really matters' from what is on offer. As with a cook-book, I am attracted to certain kinds of recipe on the basis of what I know I like, or will probably like, and what I know I will be able to do, or will probably be able to do.

One Chinese recipe leapt to my eyes from a large collection. It was for prawns in batter, with sesame seeds and honey. For a time, this became a day-off special, until I began to realize the number of calories it contained. The 'information' had been selected – and filtered – on the grounds of taste and availability of ingredients, and in this case had certainly travelled 'from one end of the earth to another'.

All this indicates that when we are overloaded, inner mechanisms in the mind and memory operate as a kind of defence, rather like the digestive process when too much food, or food that is too unfamiliar, is suddenly eaten. And already, an important distinction is being made between *knowledge*, which is about the acquisition of facts, and *wisdom*, which is about being able to make right judgements in matters relating to life and conduct. A computer print-out can give me lots of information to try to know well, but only wisdom will enable me to discern not the facts, but 'the facts behind the facts'. Wisdom and knowledge are, therefore, frequently linked in all the world religions. Both are needed. But it looks very much as if wisdom plays second fiddle to knowledge in today's lavish spread of information on just about anything. Knowledge, at the end of the day, lives on the surface, because the more facts and data are acquired, the more superficial we become. Wisdom, on the other hand, takes us into the depths. It requires patience – a bit of 'watching and waiting'. And that is why, in the biblical tradition, whereas knowledge is never applied directly to God in the same way, though it is one of his gifts, wisdom *is*. When I was installed as Bishop of Portsmouth before Christmas 1995, I prayed for wisdom, and even asked the cathedral organist if he would write a setting for the Wisdom Antiphon for the choir to sing at the service. The resulting music fitted well, for there were notes of a transcendent quality as well as indication of sheer human struggle. All of which was very appropriate for Advent, the season of watching and waiting upon the God who is Wisdom, and the giver of knowledge.

'O Wisdom', prays the Church late every Advent. In words inspired by the opening words of the great Hymn to Wisdom well into the Book of Ecclesiasticus, which forms the centre-piece of that late Jewish work (Eccles. 24.3–7), we find our-selves looking at the origin and nature of Wisdom. Then we invoke Wisdom in terms of her *ubiquity* – she is everywhere, as the Wisdom of Solomon teaches (Wisd. 8.1). Both these books belong to the Jewish Apocrypha, which means that their canonical status is not universally acknowledged. How-ever, that need not prevent us from using these sacred texts in the liturgy in the way they have been blended together to form this antiphon. Whereas Ecclesiasticus on its own terms sees wisdom as a gift from God, the Book of Wisdom goes one stage further in viewing her as a kind of person separate from but derived from God. No wonder Wisdom came to be applied by early Christian writers to the third person of the Holy Spirit, feminine imagery and all. But here she is applied to God himself: not specifically at the Christmas festival, but in the mystery of Advent. The Book of Wisdom teaches that a wise king prays for this divine attribute, not because she is everywhere, but because she comes from God and is of God; her origins explain her ubiquity, not the other way round. It is as if wisdom can be applied to everything – including how to use stem-cells 'wisely' in medical research, in order to save lives that would otherwise be lost.

Wisdom sees deeply and refuses to skate over the surface. Moreover, wisdom *speaks* – 'from the mouth of the Lord'. Wisdom also holds things together. One of the consequences of the professionalization of theology in recent centuries – aided and abetted by information technology – has been the fragmentation of knowledge. I remember a close friend who was a brilliant scholar with all the caution of the real aca-demic, who always began the reply to any question I put to him with the words, 'Oh, but that is not quite my speciality.' In a sense that was always true. But I longed to hit the jack-pot and ask him about something that was! The best theology resists the tendency to be over-compartmentalized, and is able to see things whole. The Wisdom tradition began long before the Apocryphal books were written, for we can see traces of its combination of faith and practical application in such places as the Book of Ruth, on the one hand, where a plain novel with central characters tells us of the virtues of fidelity in times of difficulty, and throughout the Psalms, where, on the other hand, we are taught such truths as the fact that 'the fear of the Lord is the beginning of Wisdom' (Ps. 111.10) and that we should apply our hearts to wisdom (Ps. 90.12).

It would take too long to rehearse the extent of the 'Wisdom tradition' in the Bible – just as it would take too long to single out particular theological writers who demonstrate what is sometimes called 'sapiential theology', theology that holds things together, and sees things whole. One obvious example from Anglican tradition in the late sixteenth century is Richard Hooker, whom Dan Hardy identifies as embodying a characteristic of English theology within the lifetime of the Reformation itself.[1] Hardy regards Hooker as pioneering a method of doing theology that was neither bound exclusively by the claims of Scripture (like much Reformed teaching at the time) nor tied to the skirts of church tradition (as with Roman Catholicism at the time). Instead, God was seen as the author of certain 'laws', or norms, bound up in nature, including human nature operating in the context of its graceful encounter with God himself as forgiver and inspirer. This placed on the Church of any time, the community of believers, the task of forming 'right judgements' (to echo the Collect for Pentecost) over what has been inherited and how it might develop.

Hooker's *Laws of Ecclesiastical Polity* was written towards the end of his life. Volume V was intended to be a defence of the English Prayer Book – though it is much more – and it appeared in 1597. In the section devoted to the need for a Church Year, which begins with a glorious passage which states that 'the substance of God alone is infinite and hath no kind of limitation', Hooker applies this 'law' to the specifics of worship and the seasons:

All things whatsoever having their time, the works of God have always that time which is seasonablest and fittest for them. His works are some ordinary, some more rare, all worthy of observation, but not all of like necessity to be often remembered, they all have their times, but they do not all add the same estimation and glory to the times wherein they are. For as God by being every where yet doth not give unto all places one and the same degree of holiness, so neither one and the same dignity to all times by working in all . . .

No doubt as God's extraordinary presence hath hallowed and sanctified certain places, so they are his extraordinary works that have truly and worthily advanced certain times, for which cause they ought to be with all men that honour God more holy than other days.[2]

Space precluded Hooker from a specific discussion of a great deal of the Church Year, the Calendar included. But perhaps that is just as well, for in these grand sentences (he was not exactly a best-seller in his day) are contained a model for his approach to disputed matters. He was faced with Puritans who saw no need whatever for a Church Year, and certainly not anything like the four Sundays of Advent. Catholicism simply required adhering to the (over-)elaborate provisions of the Missal, with a far more complex Liturgical Year and Calendar than that contained in the Prayer Book. Between the lines of Hooker's treatment can be discerned a creative and constructive moderation, which is not about finding a middle way of compromising, but rather about looking for first principles. These are not primarily about human need, nor about tradition for tradition's sake. They are about God in time and eternity; God as ubiquitous, yet being celebrated for specific wonders and works, some of which are more important than others. In a later passage he maintains that the 'Year' begins with the annunciation and Nativity – was this a slip of the pen in a brief allusion to Advent? – and goes through to Easter and Pentecost, the two seasons in ancient times (as he points out) at which baptism was most fully celebrated.

Hooker is a 'sapiential', wisdom-based writer, who has the courage to articulate an overall *coherence* to things as they are. Humanity has certain God-given capacities, primarily the capacity to make right judgements in the face of confusion and difficulty, which are not to be shirked. Although he writes nothing about Advent, or much of the detail of the Liturgical Year and Calendar, we know that he has the whole picture in his mind when he talks about the ubiquity of God and the gift of worshipping him in time and place, for the many different attributes that are his. The abiding message of Hooker is that *we cannot take it all in at once*. It is not possible to celebrate the whole story of Christian faith, in all its richness and contradiction, in one fell swoop. Advent is a vital cog in the wheel of the year, because it provides a pause through which to contemplate an open space, God's open space. The fashion to overload liturgies with as much as possible runs the risk of turning worship into another form of consumer market, in which the special occasion, always festive in tone, happy in atmosphere, and perhaps a little suburban and muscular as well, becomes the norm.

There must be some way of liberating ourselves from this form of slavery in order to let Advent – with its joy, not its gloom – shine through. Collections of material such as are contained in the recent *Common Worship: Times and Seasons* provide just enough liturgical resourcing without overwhelming us.[3] Good, durable prayers can nourish not only public worship but private devotion, so that the worship we offer does not live a life of its own, divorced from everyday experience. One could even go so far as to say that wisdom is a liturgical gift, greater than knowledge of the facts, with which to discern sometimes hidden meaning. We need the wisdom to watch and wait for God, in his Coming among us at Bethlehem, but also in his Coming among us at the end of time.

How can this divine wisdom reach the whole range of religious experience in piety and devotion, as well as in public worship and liturgy? Some years ago, I suggested three 'pieties' in relation to Easter.[4] There is, first, the early 'unitive' approach, based on the Easter Vigil, which celebrates the death and resurrection in one single, lengthy liturgy, and therefore has no need of anything else before or after. Then there is the 'rememorative' piety, which we can see in such fourth-century practices as the palm procession, and the veneration of the (alleged) fragment of the true cross; here, there is symbolic action, but no conscious re-enactment, save in the reading of the Scripture passages. Third, there is 'representational' piety, which *is* about re-enactment: the medieval drama, the 'quem quaeritis', which began in the tenth century in England, provides an obvious example, with servers placing their amices over their heads in the middle of the Easter Vigil in order to act out the parts of the women going to the tomb. Other examples can be found, such as the modern custom of providing a donkey on Palm Sunday.

Unitive piety is subtle, sophisticated, holistic. Rememorative piety suggests an episodic treatment of the unfolding events. Representational piety is pictorial, populist, and enduring. Can we apply these to the Advent–Christmas package? Wisdom suggests that we can – and should. A unitive approach may be suggested by the early strand of the pre-Christmas fast, and the early strand of Christmas celebration which, at Rome, knew of only one mass, on the day itself, with the cosmic narrative of John's prologue as the Gospel reading (John 1.1–14), rather than the birth in Bethlehem (Luke 2.1–14), and with prayers reflecting that register. A rememorative approach may be suggested by the emergence of Advent in the sixth century, as primarily a season that proclaims the Second Coming. This throws the Christmas festival into a different light altogether, as it in turn accumulates two other Eucharists, one at night, with the birth-narrative and the shepherds (Luke 2.1–14), and then a third at dawn, with the shepherds going forth with the message of the birth (Luke 2.15–20).[5] There is no conscious re-enactment, but a symbolic engagement with the Scriptures, as well as a determination through the dynamic tension of Advent and Christmas that both be allowed to speak, but with Advent forcing its way through in order to prevent any notion that with Christmas we have somehow 'arrived'. A representational approach, however, brings its less sophisticated pictorial approach, with the worship of the 'Christ-Child', already being established at the time of Francis of Assisi in the early thirteenth century,[6] and a thematic approach to the Sundays of Advent (not so strong in the new lectionary), as well as a desire to 'act out' such biblical narratives as John the Baptist's preaching, or episodes from the life of St Nicholas.

Much as the liturgical purist opts for the rememorative approach, and derides the representational, it must be admitted that in a battle between the two the representationalists will always win, because they are nearer popular piety. As Hooker reminded us, God can be celebrated in many different ways, and they are not all of equal importance. An era of liturgical revision may well want to get rid of certain things, like 'Stir up' Sunday in order to make way for Christ the King, or Bible Sunday in order to provide further ground for John the Baptist. But it will prove well nigh impossible to eradicate the kind of person who thinks and prays in terms of pictures rather than ideas. And the pictures associated with Advent are first and foremost Jesus' warnings about the end of the world (Matt. 24.1–14; Mark 13.1–8; Luke 21.5–19), and, second, the preaching of John the Baptist in the wilderness, and his relationship with the Coming Christ (Matt. 3.1–12, 11.2–11; Mark 1.1–8; John 1.19–28; Luke 3.1–6, 7–18). The first set of readings comes from the pre-Advent season, whereas the others are used on the Second and Third Sundays of Advent, in the new lectionary. And the moral of the tale is to find mechanisms and structures for letting these great truths shine out rather more than they do, in a world that is by then already inhabited by Christmas carols and the (highly pictorial, representational) Christmas crib.

The fact that these three pieties co-exist in many sections of the community needs to be recognized – and honoured. It is not a question of different types of personality, as if we were all formed in one particular mould and remained there for the rest of our lives. It is much more like a kind of fluid mixture, with some parts appealing at one time, while others come to the fore at another time and take over. I used to love the representational piety approach as a youngster, then rebelled against it, and have since returned to it, perhaps having gone through a necessary period of intellectualizing that has not gone away, but feeds other parts of my appreciative capacities. Yet Advent can speak through all three. It is a unitive, over-all truth, about the Coming God, over-arching in its majesty, and incapable of being confined to any particular approach – something of which Hooker himself would have approved. But it is also rememorative, celebrating the different episodes of that Coming God, whether we are looking for him in daily life, at Bethlehem, or at the end of time: the symbolic language of those 'Comings' speak for themselves. And it is also representational, because some of us cannot live without the pictorial in the visual – and the television age has honed this religious instinct, for good or ill.

<hr />

'O Wisdom', prays the Church. Sadly (perhaps), there are no readings from the Wisdom tradition of the Apocrypha during the pre-Advent and Advent season, which leaves us with this, the opening of the set of seven antiphons, bringing home to us the gift of wisdom as a divine attribute.[7] Knowledge may log the facts and data of God's actions and attributes into a list. It is wisdom that enables us to understand the depths of the ways he can speak to us, in so doing using the different actions and attributes which we ourselves live out each day. Those three pieties are vital clues as to how human beings are able to apprehend the saving God. But they point to more. They remind us of the importance of patience in the life of faith. The fact that we can recognize different approaches, and the fact that we have liturgical resources at our disposal, means more than ticking a box and saying that all is well.

In the plethora of liturgical resources, it is easy to be overwhelmed by the sheer amount available, and to be tempted to start all over again, inventing one's own act of worship. Sometimes these can be very creative indeed, especially when in the hands of an unusually gifted person or group of people. But for most of us, the best plan is to learn the disciplines and the shapes of what is now on offer, and to see it all as part of a living tradition. It was William Penn who warned us against decrying things simply because we do not understand them. I can think of many examples in my own life when this has been the case, when I have shown impatience in the face of good things, rich treasures, words and traditions I've not understood as immediately as the start of the television news bulletins. We need patience with the provisional, and we can't expect everything to be transparent in the same way that we yearn for bureaucratic processes to be transparent – or, indeed, the rush some local congregations get into in order to get an appointment of a new priest that is at the same time rapid *and* carried out with maximum consultation. We need to love the liturgy, and use it sparingly, letting a little go a long way, savouring the words, instead of rushing to their conclusion in order to have finished it. The 'mouth of the Most High' means words spoken by God himself. The liturgies may not exactly contain those words, but they provide a faith-based vehicle for God to speak to his people, even if how he speaks is oblique, not always obvious, and invariably challenging.

Advent, like good theology, holds all these truths together, and refuses to let them be dissipated into three discrete areas, where one moment we are waiting for Bethlehem to happen, another we are gazing at ourselves in self-obsession, agog at what Jesus might be saying to our innermost souls at this very moment, only to switch manically to the eternal perspective that somehow makes up the end of all things. It is hard to take in the truth that all three belong together. What wisdom brings to this exercise is the sheer truth that they do belong together, and the patience needed to persist with them, and with the three pieties that help us approach Advent and Christmas in such a way that God is worshipped in all his goodness, his mercy, his judgement, and his truth.

This may be what the author of the antiphon meant when those words were coined about 'ordering sweetly'. For divine wisdom above all assumes that, as in Hooker's theology, coherence underscores the lives we lead. That may be a hard truth to digest, especially in a world like ours which is dangerous in so many ways, whether one is thinking of terrorism, global warming, late-night street violence, or the often hidden sins of the boardroom, with their sometimes ruthless games of manipulation. But if God is God, then it follows that coherence is what we are meant to share, and there are foretastes of that coherence that can be experienced through life as we ordinarily know it. To order things sweetly means a coherence that is pleasant to the taste, which may mean facing up to the hard truths that Advent brings to light, but undoubtedly means a God who is *good*.

All of this has many consequences. For a start, Advent wisdom must be about perceiving prophetically, by which I mean the capacity to look at the world as it is and see beyond what is obvious and passing, in order to discern what are the eternal truths. A Church that encourages this approach is bound to run the risk of getting into trouble, of upsetting people, of being told to get back into the sanctuary and stay there. Advent perception, Advent wisdom, may lead us into areas where we have not been before, because the path taken hitherto has been one of 'safety first'. Our world struggles for a reinterpretation of human identity, what it means to be participants in anything, because so much of our social fabric is at risk, and collective trust stunted, or at least seriously diminished. To look for the Coming God could be dangerous. But wisdom, which is everywhere, which comes from the mouth of God, and which orders sweetly – that is a tall order. And yet to ask such divine wisdom to 'come and teach us the way of prudence' is to lay ourselves open to such danger.

Second, Advent wisdom will inevitably be about watching and waiting. But how? In today's world, many people pride themselves on how their lives are under control, how they know what they are going to be doing next Wednesday

afternoon at 4.30 p.m., and where exactly in the supermarket they will find precisely the foodstuffs required for the
evening meal that needs to be crushed in between everyone
coming home and some going out again for (always) pressing engagements or leisure activities of one sort or another.
Wisdom means resisting all that, and seeing how another part
of the world carries out its existence. After a serious illness, I
can recall the anxious faces of fellow patients as they wait in
the clinic for what seems an eternity – but may be only a few
minutes – for the results of blood tests that could mean life or
death in the future. Will I survive? For how long is this going
to go on? Can I really cope with even more of all this watching
and waiting? The anxiety levels can be palpable. But *this* is the
kind of uncontrolled world inhabited by a larger proportion
of the human race than many of us imagine. Advent wisdom
lives in that world, and watches and waits with it, in faith and
in hope. It prefers that real world to the glorious fantasies of
the other world of frenetic activism, living on the surface, just
'being busy'.

Then there is a third dimension, which might be called
divine passivity. Some years ago W. H. Vanstone wrote a small
book, entitled *The Stature of Waiting*, in which he looks at the
figure of Christ going forth to be betrayed and crucified, re-
ceiver of suffering, and at the same time instrument and agent
of God. Then he applies these observations to ourselves, as
we not only watch and wait with patience, but go one step
further: we receive from God, and so, far from becoming less
than ourselves in a demeaning manner, we become more than
ourselves, recipients of the divine gifts always intended for us
through that very watching and waiting. This is how the book
ends:

> As he waits in the future, increasingly dependent on systems
> and machines, on organization and technology, on medi-
> cal support and social provision, [man] will in no sense be
> deprived of his high calling – that of standing beside God
> and receiving into the transforming mirror of his conscious-

ness what the world really is. Whenever he so stands, in the future as in the past and present, man will be a figure of unique and almost unbelievable dignity.[8]

## Notes

1 See the essay by Daniel E. Hardy, 'Theology through Philosophy: The Vision of English Theology', in David F. Ford (ed.), *The Modern Theologians* (Vol. II) (Oxford: Blackwell, 1989), pp. 30ff.

2 Richard Hooker, *Laws of Ecclesiastical Polity*, Book V, Ch. lxix.3.

3 See *Common Worship: Times and Seasons*, pp. 32–60; this material is largely a revision of what appeared in *The Promise of His Glory: Services and Prayers for the Season from All Saints to Candlemas* (London: Mowbray, 1990), pp. 91–144.

4 See the discussion of these areas in relation to Holy Week and Easter in Kenneth Stevenson, *Jerusalem Revisited: The Liturgical Meaning of Holy Week* (Washington: Pastoral Press, 1988), pp. 9–12.

5 See Cowley, *Advent*, pp. 83–6.

6 See John Gunstone, *Christmas and Epiphany* (Studies in Christian Worship IX) (Leighton Buzzard: Faith Press, 1967), pp. 104–06.

7 A disputed point in some areas of early Christian literature, it is nonetheless a commonplace for describing some kind of companion of God; see Larry W. Hurtado, *Lord Jesus Christ: Devotion to Jesus in Earliest Christianity* (Grand Rapids: Eerdmans, 2003), p. 125.

8 W. H. Vanstone, *The Stature of Waiting* (London: Darton, Longman & Todd, 1982), p. 115.

# 2

# *Lord*

## O Adonai

*O Adonai, and leader of the House of Israel,*
*who appeared to Moses in the fire of the burning bush*
*and gave him the Law at Sinai:*
*Come and redeem us with an outstretched arm.*

When a parish is seeking a new priest, many requests are often
made. Apart from wanting the archangel Gabriel, aged 36,
with 2.5 children, who is a wow with the young, an enthusiast
for the elderly, 'comfortable' with all kinds of worship, and a
good community presence, there is a not infrequent undercur-
rent about 'strong leadership'. And much of this can get trans-
ferred to an advertisement in the church press. The truth of
the matter is that such a quest invariably leads to disappointment. No one can fulfil all these expectations, and certainly
not the call for such apparently strong leadership – which usually means fitting in exactly with the prejudices of the person
articulating such a desire. Yes, it's good to have a parson who
knows their mind. But unless that 'strong leadership' is something other than what is often initially desired, the quest will
probably end in failure.

Part of the problem is that the churches today are facing
many difficulties that they have not faced before. Today's challenges are bound to differ from those of a century ago. The
kind of fragmentation of local communities caused by such
factors as family break-ups, week-end employment and the in-

crease in the leisure industry put pressure on what a local congregation can do on a Sunday. Then there are public debates
in which the Church fails to speak with a single, united voice,
with Bishops even daring not to speak all the same way – which
plays straight into the hands of those who seek moral certainties where some of us are unable always to find them. The
Church is often expected to have definite views on what might
be called the 'morally obvious' (what happens in the bedroom)
instead of looking further afield for other less obvious avenues
for moral exploration and comment, like going to war with
Iraq, passing laws that deprive us of our human rights, or fail-
ing to see an oil-slick as a sin against the environment. It is all
of a piece with a Church that is striving to be faithful to her
inheritance, yet at the same time wanting to take a fresh look
at issues that have been around for some time, and which our
age refuses to ignore.

The call for 'strong leadership' is partly fed by one of the
most serious dynamics in the life of any institution – anger.
Anger feeds on fear, and is hardly an Advent virtue when
it translates itself into a communal angst about everything.
Many of the letters written to newspapers – and not a few
articles by religious journalists – reflect a deep-down disappointment that the churches are not performing well enough,
and claim that what we need are bishops and other leaders
who will really 'speak out', preferably echoing the line taken
by the newspaper concerned. I was once taken to task because
one of the clergy in the diocese wasn't at the altar standing
to attention on 11 November at 11.00 a.m. on the dot for the
Armistice Day silence. I gently but firmly reminded the person
concerned that it was a Tuesday, and then told him just what
the previous Sunday had been like for that cleric, as he ran
from pillar to post, celebrating the Eucharist here, doing the
Act of Remembrance there, and fitting in a marriage interview
somewhere else. Projection is an easy option indeed.

The culture of complaining often turns the Church into a
mixture of a punch-bag for everyone else to practise on, and
a supermarket where they can come and go as they please,

always insisting on exactly what they want. Yet 'strong leadership' might conceivably be about challenging some of this nonsense, and getting people together in order to work out a strategy about how they can be the community of faith in a much-changing world – where some of the changes, such as support for the elderly and minority rights, are for the better. Leadership in Christian terms must be about participation – in the life of God in our midst. If God is what we want (and need), then the constant preoccupation with the mechanics of our religion as if nothing else mattered is going to get in the way.

It is something of a comfort that – unsurprisingly – much the same kind of projection occupies our political scene. Low turnouts at elections continue to be a source of worry to our politicians (it is regularly calculated that many more people go to carol services each year than vote in local elections!), especially among the young, who increasingly learn about the news not from the oft-repeated bulletins on television but through watching comedy programmes. Moreover, the young appear to be more interested in issues than in party politics – which probably helps to explain the somewhat tardy way in which the mainstream political parties have embraced the 'Green agenda'. Politicians, moreover, are apt to think that people discuss politics a great deal more than they do, just as clergy are apt to think that the latest church controversy occupies the minds of the faithful throughout every hour of every day.

Part of the answer to these matters, both the religious and the political, is to look not only at the cracks in the system (what are people really interested in, and why?), but also for new ways of building up and creating community life (if it's true that to be real is to be local, why not go with the flow, instead of resisting it?). Over the past decade, I have been privileged to be bishop of a small, thickly populated diocese on the south coast of England and have watched the way new initiatives, whether political, social, or church-led, have enabled people to participate in how their future is to be worked out. Sometimes this has meant getting the clergy to leave the room, because their presence can stifle debate. Sometimes this has meant cancelling the normal agenda of what are frequently quite tedious meetings, in order for people to be liberated to discuss what really matters, such as new local initiatives for mission and ministry. This has on occasion produced some tensions with the synodical system, and it has even led some congregations to be bold enough to say, 'In order to do this, which is of pressing importance, we are going to stop doing that.' Leadership can be strong when it is local, shared, and brings a community to a more realistic strategy than it had before. But leadership that follows exclusively secular models will not get us very far. The Kingdom Christ comes to inaugurate – and the Kingdom of the Advent season – is a far messier business, and one without slick, target-conscious rewards.

This is precisely how an increasing number of Christians are learning to seek God in their daily lives. It is a process that will produce a different kind of Church. Of course, it will produce a headache or two for leadership, bishops included. And there will be times when that leadership which is less local may have to intervene in order to draw things together, and provide a focus for 'communion'. But much as we like to talk about creative tension, we need also to learn that it is something inbuilt to the character of the gospel. For some people some things are going to be more important than they are for others, and that has much to do with differing temperaments, gifts, enthusiasms, and networks of relationships. That brings with it the need for prayer, and for prayer-focused ministry and mission. The following seasonal litany for Advent, which appears in *Common Worship: Daily Prayer*, provides exactly that kind of focus. We are not engaged in navel-gazing. We are trying to gaze on what God wants to do with us – one of the dimensions to Advent easily forgotten:

Jesus, servant of God,
you bring justice to the nations:
come, Lord Jesus.
You love your people with a faithful love:
come, Lord Jesus.

You were lifted up on the cross
that you might draw all people to yourself:
come, Lord Jesus.
You bring hope and joy
to those who walk in the valley and shadow of death:
come, Lord Jesus.
You have liberated us so that we might be free for ever:
come, Lord Jesus.
You, O Christ, are our justice,
our peace, and our redemption:
come, Lord Jesus.[1]

These words are flavoured with the Advent hope, and they
direct us to the kind of leadership that can be seen in the life
and death of Jesus himself, servant of God, lover of his people,
crucified for us, the source of hope and joy, the power of true
liberation, and the agent of God's justice, peace and redemption. These are Advent truths – and they come to debunk our
tired, superficial notions of leadership, whether these are based
on the widest form of acceptability (no one must be upset) or
the macho-style bully (you will do as I say, because I am here
to manage change my own way).

꿏

By what criteria should leadership be judged, and along what
lines should it be based? The image of God as 'leader' is more
subtle than any of these models, for it takes us beyond the
kinds of leadership for which we cry out, to the way in which
that leadership is applied. In modern organizational terms this
would be called something like the manual, the rule-book, the
common culture to which people are supposed to be signed up.
We are therefore taking a step beyond what we seem to want
and into a much more debated area, how the organization is
supposed to function. And here we encounter yet one more
example of our innate ambivalence: we want leadership, but
we also want the right to complain about the rules and norms

whereby we are supposed to live. The Church experiences precisely this ambivalence every day of its life. So did the People of Israel, as they moaned their way through the wilderness: every time they encountered something unexpectedly tough, it seems as if they wanted to go back to the familiar – slavery under Pharaoh in Egypt.

The Advent antiphon, 'O Adonai', takes us to Moses, the dominant figure of Israel's sacred past. *Adonai* is the Hebrew for 'Master' or 'Lord', and it comes in the plural form in order to emphasize God's majesty: its Hebraic origin is the reason why it is often not translated. But it refers to God's eternal leadership of his people. This antiphon is about encounter, for it contains echoes of the two most important encounters Moses had with God, both of them in the mountain range of Sinai. The first was before the burning bush (Ex. 3.2), and the second was when the Law was given (Ex. 24.12). The first was about his vocation, to lead the Israelites out of Egypt, away from slavery, into the Promised Land, into freedom. The second was about the means whereby they should live, which was to be no free-for-all. It forms the basis on which the whole Jewish Law was formed (the Book of Deuteronomy). It helped produce a tradition of interpretation that attempted to apply that Law in new situations, which were fraught with difficulty, hence the railings of prophets like Amos against those who are 'at ease in Zion' (Amos 6.1). Yet it also produced a spirituality that loved the Law, best summed up in the longest psalm in the Psalter, of which the following extract is typical:

Teach me, O Lord, the way of your statutes
and I shall keep it to the end.

Give me understanding, and I shall keep your law;
I shall keep it with my whole heart.

Lead me in the path of your commandments,
for therein is my delight.

Incline my heart to your testimonies
   and not to unjust gain.

Turn away my eyes lest they gaze at vanities;
   O give me life in your ways.

Confirm to your servant your promise,
   which stands for all who fear you.

Turn away the reproach which I dread,
   because your judgements are good.

See, I long for your commandments;
   in your righteousness give me life. (Ps. 119.33–40)

It is not really much of a surprise that words such a these
could be taken over without any difficulty by the Christian
Church. The Rule of Benedict directs the whole of Ps. 119 as
part of the weekly Daily Office, completing its recitation each
Sunday and Monday mainly at the 'Day Hours' (Terce, Sext
and None).[2] Modern practice often turns it into the substance
of 'Mid-day Prayer', with a few sections said each day. It can
also form an appropriate introduction (after the opening greet-
ing) to a mid-day Eucharist, when it may take rather more than
a short period of silence to flush out the cares of the morning
from overpopulated minds.

The Law invariably needs to be handled and interpreted. It
is this particular controversy that Jesus enters in his dealings
with the Pharisees, as well as other Jewish officials, who try
to trap him in argument (e.g. about paying taxes to Caesar,
Matt. 22.17ff.), or who are keen to portray him as an un-
devout Jew (e.g. because of his healing on the Sabbath, Matt.
12.10ff.). Jesus, however, sees himself as someone who has
come to fulfil the Law, not abolish it (Matt. 5.17ff.), and it is
in this light that we must 'read' the narratives of the Transfiguration (Matt. 17.1–8; Mark 9.2–8; Luke 9.28–36), where
Moses and Elijah appear, but are clearly represented now to be

subsidiary figures, and no longer of the same central importance that they once were.[3] Luke's narrative even tells us what
Jesus was talking about with them – the 'exodus' that he was
to fulfil in Jerusalem (Luke 9.31). The earliest biblical commentators, and many modern ones, do not sign up to the view
that in Moses and Elijah we have the two main representative
figures of the Law and the Prophets.[4] But there is a strong body
of opinion in antiquity and since that does indeed take that
view. Moses appears with Jesus at his Transfiguration because
he, like Elijah, represents a tradition that Jesus has come to
change and develop. The Law finds its fulfilment in Jesus himself, his person, his teaching, his ministry – and his death and
resurrection.

In a similar way, we come across the encounter between
Jewish Law and new faith in the life of St Paul. Luke provides us with no fewer than three accounts of what happened
on the road to Damascus: Acts 9.1–22, in Greek, as part of
his overall narrative of the Church's mission; Acts 22.3–21, in
Hebrew, to the Jewish crowd in Jerusalem; and Acts 26.2–18,
in Latin, to Governor Festus, together with King Agrippa and
Queen Bernice, representatives of political power. It is hard
to imagine why it is given three times, unless to emphasize its
importance and universal significance. Paul himself refers to
his conversion only obliquely and sparingly (Gal. 1.15–16; 1
Cor. 9.1, 15.8–10). But he spends more time on the relationship
between the new faith and the old. The traditional language
of conversion, which doesn't appear in these writings, helped
to give rise to a complete antithesis between the Jewish Law
as a religion of works, and Christianity as a religion of faith.
True, Paul does deal with the contrast between the old and the
new (Gal. 1.13), but he goes on to maintain that there is now
no longer Jew or Greek (Gal. 3.28). E. P. Sanders has helped
to nuance this older view by seeing rather more continuity in
Paul's religious life: he loved the Law and his upbringing as a
Pharisee at the hands of Gamaliel, but he appears to have been
looking for more.[5] The Jewish Law was not a matter of 'works'
but it required physical rites of entry, notably circumcision,

which it was impossible to demand of Gentile converts to Christianity. The Law wasn't wrong in Paul's eyes – it was a covenant that prepared the way for the new one, sealed in Jesus' blood. For Paul this created a new kind of community, centred not on what God delivered to Moses and which the People of Israel handed on – and reinterpreted – through their sacred history, but instead centred on the person of Jesus, his work and ministry.

Such an adjustment in our understanding of Paul may lead to a slightly different approach to the Damascus Road experience, namely that it was more a transformation than a 'conversion'. In case this may sound too innovative for those accustomed to speaking of radical discontinuity in the life of the Christian, perhaps we should note that Paul was a deeply religious Jew for the whole of his life up to and including his journey to Damascus. The point at issue, however, is not how to describe that experience, but how to see the very pitfalls of Christianity in our own time that Paul so lovingly and thoroughly had to deal with in his writings to the communities at Corinth, Rome and elsewhere. We are back to the rule-book, the common culture to which we are signed up – or, to put it in Christian rather than organizational terms, the person and teaching of Jesus himself. Does Advent come to transform, to transfigure the 'Law' that is what Christianity has become in our soiled hands? Jesus performs the miracle of turning the water into wine (John 2.1–11), but have we not performed (equally effectively) the reverse miracle of turning that wine back into ordinary tap-water? To what extent are our endless deliberations and decision-making processes encounters with Christ?

We have glanced at 'Law' in both the Old and New Testaments, and can perhaps see Jesus' Sermon on the Mount (Matt. 5—7) as the embodiment of this 'New Law', spoken not to a holy in-group with a religious, protective safety net around them, but instead to the whole world, with all the risks that this involves – including a readiness to see God at work in secular culture, challenging our churchiness. We need to probe a little further into that culture before we can grasp the full impact of what the Advent gospel is trying to say. For there are two threads that run through our common life that challenge much of what Christians stand for. One is the fad of modern governments towards over-legislation; and the other is litigation. It may well be that the one is the consequence of the other – but we are still faced with both. At the State Opening of Parliament, Queen Elizabeth II reads out a speech prepared by her ministers which outlines the programme for the coming parliamentary season. There is invariably a heavy legislative programme, almost certainly containing a Criminal Justice Bill, creating yet more crimes. Then at the other end of the scale, we read of people exerting their rights in order to take out law-suits of all kinds, sometimes with obvious justification (a crooked firm that won't compensate properly), and at other times, frankly, much less so. The Church reflects this climate, with people appealing to their rights more easily than they once did, perhaps because the age of deference to authority that is openly abused has gone. What may be lacking on both fronts – the legislator and the litigant – is a doctrine of restraint because 'I can, therefore I must' has taken over.

The 'new' Christian Law that captivated St Paul so powerfully in his letters to early Christian communities involved a kind of leadership that is discovered within a framework, a common culture, a tradition of preaching, teaching, worship and prayer, that binds a community together and provides it with focus, with identity, and with an outward thrust to the rest of the world. Just as leadership can stifle, so can the norms by which we are supposed to live, when these are over-applied, when they atrophy, when they stifle growth. In the next chapter, we shall be looking at some examples of major controversies where the balance of continuity and discontinuity forces Christian groups into open tension, even schism. For now, we may note in passing that Scripture, tradition and reason keep that leadership and that rule of life from being oppressive, arid and spiritually dead. The trouble is that struggling with them in flesh and blood is far more costly than writing about them in the comfort of a coal fire, in a warm room, with a lap-top computer.

༒

The antiphon opens by addressing God as Lord, and continues by evoking those two formative episodes in Moses' life, his calling and the giving of the Law, both of them formative because they are about identity. It ends by praying that God will come and redeem us with an outstretched arm – an image of God's power rooted in the Old Testament, starting with Moses (Ex. 6.6; Deut. 5.15; Ps. 135.12; Jer. 32.21), and mentioned, too, in the Magnificat's 'He has shown strength with his arm' (Luke 1.51). All this points to God's strong but gentle rule. If leadership is strongly desired, but the way it is exercised is controverted, then power is an even more difficult term to include in the Christian repertoire in today's world. Years ago, Austin Farrer preached a Christmas sermon in which he made the following observations:

> God, printing on mankind the image of his own likeness, gave us some faint resemblance of that making, that self-determining power, by which he creates the world. It is this that is heavenly in us, and it is this that is Satanic . . . We love the exercise of power in ourselves, it is the citadel of our being, our darling sin. We hate it in our neighbours, and in order to escape from it, we take a pathetic refuge in meaninglessness . . . We value slips of the tongue above sensible speech, and the muttering of sleepers above the words of wakeful men.

And he goes on:

> The universal misuse of human power has the sad effect that power, however lovingly used, is hated. To confer benefits is surely more godlike than to ask them; yet our hearts go out more easily to begging children than they do to generous

masters. We have so mishandled the sceptre of God which we have usurped, we have played providence so tyrannically to one another, that we are made incapable of loving the government of God himself or feeling the caress of an almighty kindness.

Then he says:

The power of God perplexes us, but his weakness is still all about us; this is still the engine with which he moves our minds.[6]

These are sharp words, but they have more than a ring of truth to them. God has long been described as 'omnipotent', meaning not only that he can do anything but that all power of any kind belongs ultimately to him. But our sullied hands and consciences, as individuals and as a human race, are tainted by acts of barbarism and greed, sometimes done in the name of progress. The bicentenary of the abolition of slavery in the United Kingdom, celebrated in 2007, calls to mind great Christian figures such as William Wilberforce, whose faith inspired them to work for this mighty end, in the face of many devout (and angry) Christians who used the Bible to support it. But by 1807 so many lives had been exploited, so many minds warped in the filth and mire of the slave trade, that we are still facing up to the consequences two hundred years later. Power was used in a particular way, at a particular time, when all seemed opportune. But it was a wicked, doomed project from the start; and even the most public of apologies does not mask the more subtle forms of slavery that exist today in many parts of the world, whether it is the children who die daily of the AIDS virus in Africa, or the under-class of homeless people who exist in the dark shadows of the cities of the affluent West.

Strong leadership with a misuse of power, and a scant regard for the new Christian Law, led to this miserable experiment. This leaves us with the sure and certain conclusion that

Leadership + Law + Power do not together necessarily create spiritual success. There is a deep and deadly ambiguity about power in the Christian faith. It starts at Bethlehem and ends at Calvary. It warns us not to try to run the Church as some kind of commercial success, as if it were all about bulging congregations of the strong and happy, for whom it is all a good and therapeutic hobby. Something more real may often be found in those small, struggling inner-city congregations, where the church is the only local community-builder left, and the breaking of bread each Sunday is a proclamation of power in sheer weakness.

All this is not to say that power should not be exercised, nor that every time it is called into question it is automatically wrong. That is what makes the use of power in the Church increasingly problematic, what Farrer is hinting at in the sermon just quoted. We can hate power – but there is something wrong in that as well. The 'Adonai' expressed in the Law given by Moses to the People of Israel, the Suffering Lord whom we subsequently see in the face of Jesus Christ, are Advent truths of the Coming God, in power and great glory, but a power and a glory of a very different kind than we can imagine or experience in human terms.

How can these two worlds, so near yet so different, form any kind of imaginative mutual encounter? The Christian view cannot consign the quest to the everlasting waste-bin just because of abuse in the past, and the likelihood of its continuance in the present, to say nothing of the future. Some of our talk of 'servant leadership' could give way to a more demanding exercise – a charitable, dispersed leadership, in which *all* have a proper responsibility. These are the patterns of leadership for which we must watch and wait, as the New Israel, the community of the new covenant, sealed in Christ's blood. Perhaps we need to speak less about ministerial leadership and more of priesthood, the priesthood of the whole Church, as the dynamic mess into which we are grafted, for finding direction (where we should go), context (how we should travel) and sustenance (what we should take with us).

And that takes us back not to ordination but to the font. A baptismal understanding of the Church is what the contemporary Christian community frequently proclaims. What Advent does as we look for the Coming Lord is to help us unpack some of the terminology of hierarchy, so that it can be seen as essentially relational, in the priestly Body of Christ. Episcopacy is about oversight, by someone of other people. The presbyterate is about eldership, of certain people standing in a relationship of being 'older' than others, which implies difference. The diaconate is about service, of herald 'go-betweens' in the community of faith – and outside it as well. We can also take these terms a stage further and say that each of them points to something deep in the nature of God, in oversight, eldership and service. Such a pattern is more likely than any other to keep leadership, law and power in check, so that when we pray the words, 'come and redeem us with an outstretched arm', the personal touch of God of which Farrer was speaking takes on a divine-human form.

Baptism is indeed where all our struggles with leadership, law and power begin. In the seasonal provision for baptism in the period following All Saints' Day in *Common Worship* comes the following blessing of the water, rich in themes from Israel's and the Church's sacred past:

> Lord of the heavens,
> we bless your name for all your servants
> who have been a sign of your grace through the ages.
>
> You delivered Noah from the waters of destruction;
> you divided the waters of the sea
> and by the hand of Moses
> you led your people from slavery
> into the Promised Land.
>
> You made a new covenant in the blood of your Son,
> that all who confess his name
> may, by the Holy Spirit,

enter the covenant of grace,
receive a pledge of the kingdom of heaven,
and share in the divine nature.

Fill these waters, we pray, with the power of that same
   Spirit,
that all who enter them may be reborn
and rise from the grave
to new life in Christ.

As the apostles and prophets, the confessors and martyrs,
faithfully served you in their generation,
may we be built into an eternal dwelling for you,
through Jesus Christ Our Lord,
to whom with you and the Holy Spirit
be honour and glory, now and for ever. Amen.[7]

## Notes

1 *Common Worship: Daily Prayer* (London: Church House Publishing, 2005), p. 388.

2 Timothy Fry (ed.), *The Rule of St Benedict in English* (Collegeville: Liturgical Press, 1982), pp. 45–6.

3 See Kenneth W. Stevenson, *Rooted in Detachment: Living the Transfiguration* (London: Darton, Longman & Todd, 2007), pp. 64–80.

4 See Dorothy Lee, *Transfiguration* (New Century Theology) (London: Continuum, 2004), pp. 18f.

5 E. P. Sanders, *Paul and Palestinian Judaism: A Comparison of Patterns of Religion* (Philadelphia: Fortress Press, 1977).

6 Austin Farrer, *Said or Sung: An Arrangement of Homily and Verse* (London: Faith Press, 1964), pp. 33, 34, 36.

7 *Common Worship: Christian Initiation* (London: Church House Publishing, 2006), p. 163.

# 3

# Root of Jesse

*O Radix Jesse*

*O Root of Jesse, standing as a sign among the peoples;*
*before you all kings will shut their mouths;*
*to you the nations will make their prayer:*
*come and deliver us and delay no longer.*

*Who Do You Think You Are?* is the title of a series of television programmes featuring celebrities searching for their
family roots. Viewers are treated to the prospect of figures
such as the actress Barbara Windsor and the celebrity Ian His-
lop being helped by local historians and genealogists to find
out their family origins. In an age where a sense of common
memory has experienced considerable dislocation – for various
reasons such as social mobility – we have the opportunity, if
only by proxy, to delve into the past and see how things fitted
together. It's sometimes said that interest in family history is
an affliction of middle age, or at any rate advancing years. I
once had to make a speech about what my ancestors were up
to 200 years ago, and spoke about a firm of cloth merchants in
Stirling and a collection of Danish pastors.

How we handle the past can, of course, be both a blessing and a curse. The 'heritage' industry makes us more aware
of what the past was supposed to be like, with theme parks
and historical re-creations. That sometimes means the enthusiasts who dress up in historically accurate military uniforms
in order to re-fight some of the battles of the past. 'Heritage'

is first and foremost about making the past more immediate to us than it usually is. Our cathedrals often have to give a gentle nod in this direction, if only to tell us what it was like to be one of those medieval monks who took part in building the place those centuries ago, complete with plainsong music to provide the right ambience.

It can be a blessing, if it leads on to other things, and is not too heavy-handed. What made the monks of Durham erect such a huge cathedral? What made the local Augustinian canons build a chapel to Thomas of Canterbury in Portsmouth so soon after the saint's martyrdom? But it can be just as much of a curse. Contemporary culture can easily lump the Christian Church together with the heritage industry, to attract tourists to ancient places of worship in the same way that they might want to see Buckingham Palace or the Tower of London. And acid rain in the atmosphere means that running a cathedral is an expensive business, with stonework being repaired nearly all the time.

Buildings and people together constitute a sense of place.[1] And by 'place' I mean more than the sum total of the stonework, the lead on the roof, the organ-pipes, even the lighting and the microphone system. By place I mean the whole experience of walking into a building, whether on my own or with a group of other people, either forming a set of experiences in that very instant, or else picking up from where I left off the last time I went there. Locating myself in space and time often means sacred space, space that has been prayed in and both loved and nurtured. A society that cuts itself off from the past, whether deliberately or by accident, soon discovers that it lacks important points of reference. Contemporary Europe is almost too full of the outward signs of a strong and powerful Christian past, yet in many places visible Christianity is increasingly confined to the big, special occasion, and the day-by-day prayer of the community sustained by a few, whether in a French monastery or by a group of laypeople in an English country village.

In the 'Root of Jesse' we come to the first of the (only two)

Advent antiphons that do not invoke qualities or ideals, but mention *people*. For any devout Jew mention of the 'Root of Jesse' takes the community right back to the roots of its monarchy, with the anointing by Samuel of David, youngest son of Jesse (1 Sam. 16.1–23). The image of the Davidic ruler was so strong in the collective memory of the People of Israel that it signalled almost a 'back to basics' time of harmony, peace and goodwill. Nothing is necessarily mentioned of the discontinuity implied by David's anointing, as it meant the overthrow of Saul, who had proved himself unfit to carry on; nor did it mean bringing into the picture David's obvious faults, such as his adultery with Bathsheba (2 Sam. 11.1–27a). Perhaps these episodes helped make David 'real' in the eyes of the people, as do some of the peccadilloes of our leaders today.

Delving into Israel's sacred past in this way is about using symbolic characters in order to express a yearning for something new and different. The line of David (Isa. 11.10) locates Israel's history in a place and a person, like the rest of the antiphon, which refers to Egypt (Isa. 51.42) and the nations making their prayer to God (Isa. 52.53), because of a new awareness that develops in the latter part of Isaiah about Israel's role and being, to which we shall return later. The mere mention of David, like the heritage industry, is a double-edged sword: it can mean complacency about the past, or it can mean challenge in relation to the future.

The past, then, must not be played with. It needs to be *handled*. And that brings us to another negative dynamic in the life of any community – nostalgia. We need to know about the past in order to honour it, but once it becomes definitive, normative, excluding any genuine development, then the community's life is in danger. I can study the past, whether it is the theologians of the first centuries, the liturgies of the middle ages, or the preachers of the seventeenth century. But the moment they become more important to me than the life I try to lead now, the working of the social and political systems, indeed the Church itself, in all her weaknesses and controversies, then I can say goodbye to any grasp of tradition as a living thing, a dynamism – which is not determined by the past, but is in reality driven by what has gone before into a future that is always uncertain.

I come across nostalgia a great deal, people who talk in terms of their own 'root of Jesse' as if what happened a long time ago is all that mattered. Enthusiasts for the old English Prayer Book are not always like that, but a few of them are, especially when what they say about how millions of people pray today is not untinged with a bit of old-fashioned snobbery. 'Oh that everything were like how it once was!' I hear them say. And it is hard for the rest of us not to see in their view of the Church some kind of heritage exercise.

For example, I love listening to Choral Evensong on the radio, with an occasional smile at the rich voices that declaim parts of the Bible in the lessons, or the studied detachment of the way in which the prayers are sometimes read. It is part of the 'root of Jesse' of historic Anglicanism. But I also know what it is like to struggle into a small room in a block of flats to give an elderly person Holy Communion when debates about the aesthetics of which rite I am supposed to use are not quite at the forefront of my mind.[2] The other side of the coin is when one is faced with a cleric or worship-leader doing their best to discard everything that has gone before, trying to be as informal and casual as at all possible (in the most sophisticated chat-show style). Catchwords and expressions such as 'we just pray' abound, acting as semaphore signals, or so it seems, for the properly inculturated, and irritants to the rest of us. Of course I exaggerate, but in order to make a point – about having the courage to blend the old with the new, of being a 'both-and' church, rather than an 'either-or' gathering where fundamentalism in faith is matched by a complete open-endedness in worship, or a personal DIY theology somehow fed on the supposed matchless prose of the Tudor era. We really do need a sense of proportion about some of these debates, and to realize that, as with furnishing a home, there are some bits that fit better into one room than another, especially when different generations are involved.

To 'handle' the past means avoiding the different forms of purism that polarize discussion and prevent us from applying that important maxim – it's our job to *use* the liturgy, instead of debating it all the time. Advent provides many examples, not least in the Collect for the First Sunday, which was composed at the Reformation, and which sets the tone for the whole season:

Almighty God,
give us grace to cast away the works of darkness
and to put on the armour of light,
now in the time of this mortal life,
in which your Son Jesus Christ came to us in great humility;
that on the last day,
when he shall come again in his glorious majesty
to judge the living and the dead,
we may rise to the life immortal;
through him who is alive and reigns with you,
in the unity of the Holy Spirit,
one God, now and for ever.[3]

This prayer, with its echoes of Paul's letters, the most overt being the reference to the works of darkness (Rom. 13.12), places us firmly in time and space, but in such a way that we are made to be aware of our own need of salvation, starting with repentance and the work of grace in our lives, and moving on to an awareness of Christ's Coming 'in great humility' at Bethlehem, and his second coming to judge the world. We are thus faced with all three 'comings' of Christ – in daily life, at his birth, at the end of time. All three matter. None is mythological. We need the language of poetry to describe the end of the world, Jesus coming on clouds, and much else besides. We certainly use it in many a Christmas carol. And we also need it when we are trying to put into words some of the depths and heights of our own experience. This prayer is, therefore, about handling history – neither being enslaved by it, nor forgetting it. It is not about the sum total of individual parts to our collective life but about what the whole picture means. For it is that which matters most, whether we are speaking of daily discipleship, getting ready to celebrate Christmas, or contemplating the reality of what will come at the end. Advent sees life whole – and that is a secure base from which to handle history, seeing it in perspective, ready to see the hand of God in how we handle it, and ready, too, to take the risks involved in pruning back, doing (and saying) less, and making a little go a long way.

လ•ာ•

The main sources of the antiphon are Isaiah, both from the early part, which is made up mainly of specific prophecies addressed to the People of Israel, and from the later part, which reflects Israel's new situation, when all seems to be lost, and God – frequently addressed in the prophecies – is able to break through with a message of hope. Thus we have the 'Root of Jesse' (Isa. 11.10), which those familiar with Isaiah would have recognized as coming straight after the sevenfold gifts of the Spirit which will rest on the 'shoot . . . from the stock of Jesse' (Isa. 11.1–3). Around the sixth century, when these antiphons were probably being composed, it formed a prayer that followed baptism. But by the later middle ages, the end of the baptismal rite had become the rite of confirmation – where it is to this day:

> . . . The Spirit of wisdom and understanding,
> the Spirit of counsel and might,
> the Spirit of knowledge and the fear of the Lord.
> His delight shall be in the fear of the Lord. (Isa. 11.2–3a)

Other attributes follow, including a vision of a new age, in which the wolf lies down with the lamb, and the nursling child plays with the asp (Isa. 11.6, 8). When all this takes place, people will see the 'Root of Jesse' as a sign for everyone – not just the holy and devout, the chosen few.

The sources now shift to the middle part of Isaiah, what is often called 'Second Isaiah', because it seems to date from a later time. We have moved from the last third of the eighth century BC, when both the northern and southern kingdoms that made up the old Israel were under threat, to the middle of the sixth century, the time of the exile in Babylon. Two images come to mind. The first is of the Egyptians, Ethiopians and Sabaeans bowing down before the Lord (Isa. 45.14). The second is of the nations shutting their mouths before him (Isa. 52.15). The first is typical of this part of Isaiah – an increasing awareness of Israel's destiny in relation to other nations. The second comes from that part of Isaiah concerned with developing the personality and role of the 'servant of God', disfigured and rejected (as here), but also vindicated by events (Isa. 52.13–15); it is part of a passage usually linked with the passion, and read on Good Friday, but eminently suited to Advent, because it proclaims the cost of the Coming One.

We can afford to make much of this. For not only does the subtle interweaving of texts take us into a questioning, less secure hinterland of biblical context, but it also causes us to pause and consider what this hinterland says today. From the earlier part of Isaiah, when things could – just – carry on as they had done, split monarchy and all, we are in a very different world, where the two kingdoms have been taken over, the people deported, and some basic assumptions about the call of Israel have (seemingly) been discarded. Where is God to be found in the face of such a catastrophe? Isaiah's answer is a message of hope – fed on a renewal of faith. God does not need one particular place (Jerusalem) for his people to love and worship him. The good old days of the single monarchy, exemplified by David, followed by the building of the temple under his son, Solomon, have gone for ever. We are in a completely new situation, terrifying, insecure, uncertain. But God still is God.

From time to time I have been present at gatherings when this very same atmosphere of fear and anxiety has taken over. It is as if the sevenfold gifts of the Spirit did not exist, and all we have to go on is a kind of private agreement with the Lord whereby we will only serve him as long as the old, tried and familiar ways hold sway. Dare we dream of a time when all kings will indeed shut their mouths, whether from Egypt, Ethiopia, Saba, or any of the modern secular equivalents, whether it is an all-too powerful newspaper magnate, a multinational corporation trying to look kinder to the poor of the Third World than they really are, or a malign influence in the Church that is always looking back to the past? Could it just be possible that the superpowers that dominate our lives might even be silent in the face of the Lord of all time and eternity?

These are the hopes and fears that continue to afflict the human race – and the Church as well. We love to play the nostalgia game, looking back to the golden age that never was (David had clay feet, large Victorian church buildings were seldom full of people), as we re-write history in order to place ourselves in as negative a light as possible. Our search for God, yet again, takes the form of the mechanical and the superficial, as if everything could be changed overnight, *if only* things were exactly as we want them, and the Church run exactly along the lines of what we 'feel called' to do. Instead, our search for God should start where Isaiah finds him, in the difficulties, the catastrophes themselves.

It is no coincidence that the majority of Old Testament readings in the new lectionary provisions for Advent should come from Isaiah, especially in Years A and B. In the former, we start on Advent 1 with the mountain of the Lord higher than any other (Isa. 2.1–5), continue with the shoot of Jesse (Isa. 11.1–10) and the song of the wilderness (Isa. 35.1–10), and end on Advent 4 with the young woman with child (Isa. 7.10–16). Year B has a more dramatic selection: the prophet imploring God to tear open the heavens and come down (Isa. 64.1–9) on Advent 1, the famous passage about comforting the people (Isa. 40.1–11) on Advent 2, and the anointing by the Spirit of the Lord (Isa. 61.1–4, 8–11) on Advent 3. (Advent 4 has 2 Sam. 7.7–11, 16, Nathan telling David to build a house for the Lord – a text often used to point to the incarnation.)

Isaiah, whether drunk neat as in these lections, or blended together in sips as in the antiphon, wrestles with the question of what to do when everything around us seems to have fallen to pieces. And this antiphon ends less patiently than the others – 'do not delay'. Patrick Cowley remarks that if 'Alleluia' is the Easter refrain, 'Come' is assuredly the song of Advent.[4] There is an inherent impatience about Advent – if, that is, we are sufficiently uncomfortable and dissatisfied with life as it is. Far too often we ask each other if we are 'comfortable' with this or that procedure, this or that prayer or order of service, as if Jesus were a domestic pet, whose only role is to cosy up to us and be stroked in a warm, untroubled room. 'If you haven't got any problems,' runs the poster outside a university chaplaincy, 'come inside and we'll give you some!' Uncomfortable and dissatisfied as we are supposed to be, the life of faith should never indulge in spiritual complacency, for that is to suggest that we can rule Advent out, or turn it into another phase that we go through, like motions in a dance that mean nothing and matter even less.

We must read between the lines of the antiphon and see there lightly concealed another summary of the gospel: the root of Jesse, taking us back to the king of old; the great powers, the people and influences who somehow matter, who will shut their mouths (a real sign of impotence in today's world) and bow down (a contradiction of everything that makes up our culture of autonomy at all costs). These are the ingredients of the Coming Christ, who turns old patterns of leadership and monarchy into a new way of shepherding the flock, whose teaching dumbfounds his hearers, and whose death brings us all to our knees. It says something of the ingenuity of the author of this antiphon that these shadows hover in the background, suggesting from old-established forms and structures what the new and eternal Coming One will be like.

The 'Root of Jesse' confronts us with the balance between continuity and discontinuity. How do we ask the Lord to 'come', and square that request with the reality of history? To that question there are many answers. We shall look at three of them briefly.

First, to handle tradition means being prepared to look at it in a fresh light, which is primarily in terms of our search for God. Years ago, in a Retreat address, Evelyn Underhill made the following remarks, which have a wider application as well:

What does union with God mean? It is not a nice feeling we get in devout moments. That may or may not be a by-product of union – probably not. It can never be its substance. Union with God means every bit of our human nature transfigured in Christ, woven up into His creative life and activity, absorbed into His redeeming purpose, heart, soul, mind and strength. Each time it happens it means that one of God's creatures has achieved its destiny.

And she goes on to define what kind of prayer emanates from those priorities:

What they ask from us on our side and from our prayer is a very great simplicity, self-oblivion, dependence and suppleness, a willingness and readiness to respond to life where it finds us and to wait, to grow and change, not according to our preconceived notions and ideas of pace, but according to the overruling Will and Pace of God.[5]

To handle tradition freshly is something we do all the time, and as a community we would be the better for realizing just that. It comes at those crunch points in any community, whether it is in the search for a new pastor, being ready to share a priest with another congregation and asking questions about shared ministry in the future, looking prayerfully for ordinands, finding a youth leader (the Church of England employs more of these than any other organization), an organist or co-ordinator of the music group, or someone to carry out the sometimes thankless responsibilities of churchwarden. What they want and the kind of priorities they identify for their communities is but one more way of handling what has been inherited. And it is more than likely to help the community think about what they are trying to do and be, sometimes at a far deeper level than has happened before. Underhill's words about 'self-oblivion' have a ring of truth to them.

Second, continuity and discontinuity rear their heads in the major controversies of the day. It sometimes takes some energy on my part to engage with them, perhaps because I am not alone in being somewhat wearied by polarized positions, to say nothing of the amount of time that they nearly always take up. I remember, the day when my appointment to Portsmouth was announced, running the gauntlet of a series of television interviews. One of them began with the words, 'What about women clergy and gays?' to which I replied (rather facetiously) 'What a surprise to be asked that question!'

It is important that we recognize first and foremost that the Church has known controversy from the very start. The Acts of the Apostles is frequently held up as a tale of Church growth – which indeed it is. But it also chronicles the beginnings of the collapse of the Church in Jerusalem (Acts 12.2), and an ongoing and very bitter row about whether Gentile converts should have to be circumcised or not; and indeed, reading between the lines, it would appear that this matter was not easily or immediately settled. Our collective memory of conflict, in spite of the fact that the central symbol of our faith is a cross, continues to be somewhat limited. This does not reduce the heat in some quarters about the gender of those ordained and what we do about a society that is more open in its discussion about sexuality and lifestyle. I grew up against women's ordination and unable to discuss homosexuality. Since then I have made the journey into being strongly in favour of the one, and accepting of the other. These journeys have yet to be made by others. I regret the pain that such questions cause within the worldwide Church. I regret, too, the pain that the views stated here may cause to those who do not share them, although I know that others will be relieved to read them.

To ordain women as deacons, presbyters, bishops, is an obvious development in the Church, which I can reduce to the simple formula taught me some years ago by a retired Roman Catholic professor: 'If you are going to baptize women, you must be prepared to ordain them.' I am encouraged towards this position by the radical way in which the New Testament treats women, not least how Jesus addresses the Samaritan woman at the well in public (John 4.7), flouting custom that he should do no such thing. Long before debates about women's ordination were even thought of, Maximus, who was Bishop of Turin in the first part of the fifth century, preached a sermon on this very text (John 4.7ff.), powerfully endorsing her place in the redeemed community: 'Abandoning her pitcher she brings not water but grace back to the city. She seems, indeed, to return without a burden, but she returns full of holiness.'[6]

When it comes to the debate about sexuality, two Scripture passages attract attention. To apply the 'Holiness Code' of Leviticus when it deals with sexual prohibitions (Lev. 18.1–30) exclusively in the direction of homosexual practice is to take a very partial view of the evidence. Later on, it directs that adulterers be put to death (Lev. 20.10) and all blasphemers similarly treated by being stoned (Lev. 24.14). Ironically, it was for blasphemy that Jesus was charged by the Jews, but they wanted him crucified for political sedition, a far more lingering and painful death than being stoned. Then there is Paul's list of sins at the start of his letter to the Romans (Rom. 1.18ff.): but a case can be made for concluding that Paul is attacking the widespread practice of homosexual prostitution and pederasty – which is something different from mature same-sex relationships.

I know that these texts – and others like them – are used to support a Church that should frown on gays, or at least indulge in the inconsistent view that church members can be practising homosexuals but clergy can't (where is the baptismal ecclesiology in that?). But I find myself unmoved by such an interpretation of Scripture, and increasingly convinced that to accept mature homosexuality is a legitimate development in the Christian life. Many cannot accept this position. Generations to come will have their own painful differences that threaten to split the Church, as has happened before. At least I am in a community that is prepared to talk about the issue. Whatever one's view, at least we can agree that homophobia is wrong. I vividly recall at the 1998 Lambeth Conference a bishop from Central America defending gays on the basis of a genuine experience of love – and another bishop from somewhere else who, when pressed on the issue, admitted that gays were stoned or thrown out of their villages.

Advent tells us to handle tradition in a fresh way, starting with the prayer of self-forgetfulness. Advent speaks to us in the sharp controversies that make for continuity and discontinuity in the Church at large as well as globally. But Advent also, third, draws us into a deeper and richer understanding of the fact that the Church is present everywhere, in every single action that she performs – in spite of all our differences. Nowhere is this more forcefully expressed than in the famous 'Devotion XVII' which John Donne, a seventeenth-century Dean of St Paul's, wrote in a set of meditations during a period of serious illness in 1623, and which were published the year after. Illness – especially when it is potentially life-threatening – has a habit of underscoring what is important and identifying what is secondary. Life is never the same afterwards.

Perchance he for whom the bell tolls, may be so ill, as that he knows not it tolls for him; and perchance I may think myself so much better than I am, as that they who are about me, and see my state, may have caused it to toll for me, and I know not that. The Church is Catholic, universal, so are all her actions; all that she does, belongs to all. When she baptizes a child, that action concerns me; for that child is thereby connected to that head which is my head too, and engrafted into that body, whereof I am a member. And when she buries a man, that action concerns me: all mankind is of one author, and is one volume; when one man dies, one chapter is not torn out of the book, but translated into a better language; and every chapter must be translated; God employs several translators; some pieces are translated by age, some by sickness, some by war, some by justice; but God's hand is in every translation; and his hand shall bind up all our scattered leaves again, for that library is where every book shall lie open to one another.[7]

To watch and wait for the 'Root of Jesse' is another exercise in patience – not least a patience that enlarges our sympathies and our awareness of just how deeply we are united together by our actions and our prayers, our circumstances and our struggles.

## Notes

1 See the important study by John Inge, *A Christian Theology of Place* (Explorations in Practical, Pastoral and Empirical Theology) (Aldershot: Ashgate, 2003).

2 Cf. Alan Bennett, 'Comfortable Words', in *Writing Home* (London: Faber & Faber, 2004), p. 356 (whole essay, pp. 350–6).

3 *Common Worship: Services and Prayers for the Church of England*, p. 376.

4 Cowley, *Advent*, p. 39.

5 Evelyn Underhill, *Light of Christ* (London: Longmans, 1944), pp. 45–6.

6 Maximus of Turin, Sermon 22.2, quoted in Joel C. Elowsky (ed.), *Ancient Christian Commentary on Scripture: New Testament IV a: John 1–10* (Downers Grove: Inter-Varsity Press, 2006), p. 147.

7 John Donne, 'Devotion XVII', in John Hayward (ed.), *John Donne, Dean of St Paul's: Complete Poetry and Selected Prose* (London: Nonesuch Press, 1930), pp. 537–8; modern English spelling adopted for the sake of ease.

# 4

# Key of David

## O Clavis David

*O Key of David, and sceptre of the House of Israel;*
*you open and no one can shut; you shut and no one can open:*
*come and lead the prisoners from the prison house,*
*those who dwell in darkness and the shadow of death.*

For some people, habits are important and they become in-grained over time. I have been going to the Eucharist regularly since I was a small boy. In fact, I do not remember a time when I did not attend somewhere. Over the years, a whole range of different eucharistic experiences has been amassed in my memory. The staple diet with which I began was the quiet, early morning celebration in the presence of about a dozen people in a nineteenth-century church on the east coast of Scotland. The building was dark and often cold. The atmos-phere was quiet – no one either dared or wanted to talk be-forehand (that was left for afterwards). The service-book was anything but 'user-friendly'. It was just a mass of words, not helped by whole sections of material (those long exhortations) which were never used. There was never any sense of wanting to create a big experience out of it all. It just happened, and that was that. And it was repeated every Thursday morning, and I enjoyed going to that additional celebration during the school holidays.

But there were other, perhaps more dramatic and challeng-ing, occasions that I can remember. A camping holiday in

France took us one Sunday morning to Chartres Cathedral. This had the stunning effect of seeing that amazing building, with its magnificent medieval stained glass, in the context of living worship, and not as a tourist attraction. It was the late 1950s, so many of the changes made in the Roman Catholic liturgy had yet to come about. One sensed the clergy and ministers straining to get beyond the Latin words in order to use as much French as at all possible. An aged canon preached a powerful sermon that would have done justice to any fire-eating Methodist lay preacher. We were swept up into the service, following its shape, rather than its actual wording.

A Greek holiday in my student days furnished me with yet one more variant in this repertoire. Athens Cathedral, packed to the doors for a festal liturgy, proved a very contemporary context in which to savour the Byzantine Eucharist, with loud singing, billows of incense, and a congregation that managed to stand for the whole length of the service. There were high moments, such as when the Book of Gospels was brought in, and later on, the Great Entrance, with the eucharistic bread and wine. The proportion of people receiving communion was appreciably smaller than in the other examples I have given, but there was still a strong sense of participation – even though the language was Byzantine Greek, and not the Greek spoken today. Once again, the overall shape of the liturgy took me through what was a maze of detail, with litanies here and interventions by the choir there.

Then there was the experience of a Danish Lutheran service, which became more and more important to me as time went on because of my family roots. We worshipped mainly in Århus Cathedral, with the fine reredos behind the altar described earlier in this book. I was always struck by two things: the brightness of the interior of the building, and the valued place given to organ music, with those delicious mini-preludes and postludes improvised by the organist before and after each hymn. I relished the dignified simplicity of the service, with colourful vestments at the altar, and black gown with white ruff only in the pulpit. Choral and organ music during the distribution of communion made for a sacred moment, shared with those kneeling beside me. Once more, the overall shape of the service was familiar, and that helped me engage with the words, even if the sermon was often beyond me.

I could give many other examples, from early experiences as well as from the week-by-week visits to parishes in the diocese. I am always struck by the privilege of presiding at worship in the churches in the Portsmouth area, ranging from a rural gathering on the Isle of Wight to the more 'happy-clappy' liturgies in suburbia on the mainland. I am always struck, too, by the freshness of those who come to faith in adulthood, who have come to confirmation through an Alpha course; my own sense of personal inheritance is invariably challenged by the newness of their Christian experience. But as with my childhood, the unifying factor in all the acts of worship is that overall shape, which is just occasionally a little hard to inculcate in people's minds because of the sheer variety of what is now on offer. By contrast, the worship in my chapel is simple and austere, like its modern architecture, with its Scandinavian-style use of woodwork. People who come to my chapel often say afterwards how nourishing the simplicity of the experience often is. It may form something of a contrast with the fuss and activism that they experience elsewhere.

I suppose I could have discussed the Eucharist in relation to other of the 'O' Antiphons, because there is something of the wisdom of God about the service, as well as the Lordship of Christ, and even the balance of continuity and discontinuity that we can discern in the 'Root of Jesse'. And as for what is to come, Morning Star, King of the nations, and Emmanuel could all take their place – somehow – around the table of the Lord. But the curious theme of 'Key of David' wins through, because it raises questions about access, about discipleship today, and about issues concerning inclusion and exclusion. The Eucharist is, above all, a crucial key to the business of following Christ. Indeed, some would say that it is *the* key, because in gathering together, in sharing the Word of God, and in eating and drinking at that holy table, we are making bold statements about what we have access to, about our claims to be disciples, about being genuinely included in the meal that points us to heaven. Every Eucharist has an Advent flavour, because, in Paul's words, 'as often as you eat this bread and drink the cup, you proclaim the Lord's death until he comes' (1 Cor. 11.26).

The one thing, therefore, that the Christian cannot pretend to be is someone cut off from the past. However ordinary we may try to make the Eucharist, the words and actions have been given to us by another age, another culture, and it is a question of letting them be our own. As Rowan Williams observes in a series of lectures about the use of history, 'one of the most evident marks of Christian community is . . . the regular business of literally making our own the rhythms and vocabulary of another age.'[1]

In each of the examples just mentioned, the Eucharist is that key, whether it is the quiet, early morning celebration, transmuted into the modern setting of my chapel (perhaps despised by some purists, but remarkable in its power to survive, even if the pre-service chit-chat takes over); the grand occasion in a large historic building (it could be an English cathedral, with the military precision one associates with an Anglican procession); the delightful mixture of ancient ritual and Mediterranean popular chaos of the Orthodox liturgy (would that we could learn just a little bit of how to trust the liturgy to be itself!); or the measured atmosphere of classical Lutheranism (a culture that has given Europe so much of its finest music).

The image of the key immediately conjures up images of *access* – and the issue of *accessibility*. The quiet service, the large gathering, the Greek experience, and the Danish one – they all have their weaknesses and strengths. Not one of them can attempt to 'say it all', however much one invests in quietness and simplicity, the hustle and bustle of the big Sunday gathering, the grand and ancient style of the Byzantine liturgy, or that very

Danish occasion, in which hymnody – much of it written by national poets – was so central. There are limits to access and accessibility in each, and the Church will be wrestling with these issues, and, indeed, the proper relationship between the Eucharist and other acts of worship, until the end of time.

These questions bring back endless discussions when I was a parish priest about how to 'make' the Sunday morning Eucharist more 'accessible' to people unused to be there. As with many congregations, it was by far the best-attended service in the parish on a Sunday. As in many a modern community, that act of worship had to 'carry' almost too much. It was not fed or built up to by as much thoughtful Bible study and daily prayer as I would have liked, or the 'messy church' experiments on the edges of the Church inspired by the Fresh Expressions initiative. In much, though not all, of our talk, there seemed a mechanistic approach about 'making things accessible', as if what we were doing was something akin to giving the ten o'clock news a fresh look, instead of providing an opportunity for God, the Coming Lord, to speak on his own. In a culture that seems to want all the time to reduce highly complex matters into simple slogans, I often thought that these discussions were on a hiding-to-nothing. We could simplify the preaching – yet necessary though that often is, it might assume a facile approach on the part of the young people's groups. 'All-age worship' needs to be for all ages. We could drop the sermon altogether and provide a 'commentary' at different parts of the service – always a winner, and invariably appreciated by people who had become perhaps a bit too familiar with it all for their own comfort. We could try singing different styles of music – often the most divisive issue in a congregation, and where no one group has prior rights.

In all our endless talk about 'accessibility' providing 'access' to God, were we not in danger of playing God ourselves? Is the Church supposed to mirror contemporary culture to the extent that we allow divine worship to degenerate into something that it was never intended to be? Perhaps we were starting at the wrong end. Perhaps in all our anxiety to make it all acceptable we were missing the point. And re-writing the liturgy each week was hardly going to help, for a congregation needs rhythms and shapes and forms for worship, over and above the specific demands of a building where visibility (lighting), audibility (a sound-system) and heating (that works properly) were more important issues for the congregation than where the celebrant stood and which eucharistic prayer was to be used – to say nothing about a service-sheet that is well laid out and liberates the congregation from being faced with a library of material at the church door.

All these questions are important – but they are not all-important. The *Common Worship* Eucharist, like most modern rites in all the mainstream Churches, has an overall shape that links with the past and the present, almost worldwide. Within that framework there is an opening rite of penitence, a seasonal prayer that leads into the readings, a sermon, prayers of intercession, the preparation of the table, a eucharistic prayer, followed by communion, and the concluding prayers. We are still getting used to these varying texts and we are still learning to pray them. They are not quick disposable commodities that we can cast off when we get bored by them. They are the authorized texts of our Church. They may not be perfect, and we might well prefer texts that emanate from elsewhere (ecclesiastical tourism in an ecumenical age has its advantages). But they are meant to point us to a God who is *both* accessible *and* infinitely mysterious.

To ask everyone immediately afterwards what they thought was going on will not produce a definitive statement for a number of reasons. One person may have arrived feeling very raw after a family row, because the partner is not a church-goer. Another grudgingly turns up after a difficult week at work in the course of which they have been dismissed. Another has worked hard at the music, only to discover that a carefully planned anthem has been cancelled for no apparent reason. Yet another is an enquirer who doesn't quite know what is going on because it is so different from what they remember from a church in childhood.

David Ford remarks in a recent book, 'it is hard to overestimate the importance for Christianity of the fact that the eucharist, a pivotal locus of its identity, is a corporate practice rather than, say, an ethical code, a worldview, a set of doctrines, an institutional constitution, a book, or some distinctive feature.'[2] And he goes on to extol an approach to eucharistic theology that takes far more seriously what he calls the eucharistic 'habitus', the context of the celebration, how people sit and dress, what the building is like, styles of preaching, and much else that perhaps in the past has been dismissed as secondary. Perhaps the weaknesses of modern liturgies is how they begin and end. Gathering people together (perhaps when the building is large) at the start for a time of quiet, with some pointers to prayer, would be as effective as providing specific pointers to prayer and action at the end.

We shall never manage to unravel the Eucharist, because the Eucharist is too big for us. That truth has struck me practically every time I have attempted to preach about it, and many a time when I have strode thoughtfully back to my place after receiving the eucharistic bread and wine, the Body and Blood of Christ. I cannot define it, but I can try to describe it. And the Advent season halts me in my tracks, and prevents me from being too clear, too neat, about what it all means. I cannot make it all accessible. But I can try to be a better point of access myself, by thinking more about what I am doing, and by trying to apply it more faithfully in my daily tasks. Something of that Christ-centred truth is summed up in the Extended Preface for the first part of Advent, in the way that it points to the Coming Saviour, bringing the gift of salvation, and filling us with the right kind of confidence, confidence in God being God – no more, no less:

It is indeed right and good to give you thanks and praise,
almighty God and everlasting Father,
through Jesus Christ your Son.
For when he humbled himself to come among us in human
    flesh,

he fulfilled the plan you formed before the foundation of
  the world
to open for us the way of salvation.
Confident that your promise will be fulfilled,
we now watch for the day
when Christ our Lord will come again in glory.
And so we join our voices with angels and archangels
and with all the company of heaven
to proclaim your glory,
for ever praising you and saying:
Holy, Holy, Holy Lord . . .[3]

Points of access are important, whether they are effective
disciples, or a building that is used imaginatively. But all our
talk about access and accessibility, about being open and not
closed, eventually leads to the question of *discipleship*. This
is a much-used word, and necessarily so, because it comes to
the heart of what it is to follow Christ. Any culture, as we
hardly need reminding, has its own particular faults, and ours
is no exception. A great deal of attention in public discourse
concerns our rights as individuals, and the Church often has
its own version of these trends within its own organization
and internal discourse, as if worshippers were primarily con-
sumers who have to be kept happy. Patterns of worship often
seem to be tailor-made for particular needs and groups, who
in turn may well be likely only to turn up for what is 'for
them'. Sometimes the variations are not, at the end of the day,
all that great. This means that churches have 'on offer' what
is really rather a narrow band of worship, instead of liturgies
that function alongside the Eucharist, whether in schools or
pubs, which can speak to those on the fringe of church life,
without dumbing down the essentials of the gospel.

But there is an outward focus for discipleship which can
be equally troubling, and that is to be faced with the vast-
ness of the world and its problems, and the smallness of the

Christian presence in that sometimes quite overwhelming context. 'What must I do?' is the question we frequently ask of ourselves at the end of the Eucharist, especially after praying those words about offering ourselves 'as a living sacrifice'. But God does not call us to take on the whole world, still less to find the nearest cross and nail ourselves to it. And he certainly does not call us to be religious martyrs, determined to draw attention to ourselves as we shout from the roof tops about the latest ecclesiastical development that we fear and that (we can be sure) does not figure very much at all on the agenda of the millions of folk who have written us off as a narrow-minded group of people only interested in ourselves.

The Gospels time and again remind us of the immediacy, the 'here and now' aspects, of following Christ, those thousands of opportunities that lie on our doorsteps, all of which may relate in some way to the bigger picture, like the wide-open themes of the Advent carol services, which include one on prisoners and those who sit in darkness, aptly connecting with our antiphon, with its image of the 'prison house'. The future of our planet depends in some measure on how good stewards we are, as the species to which God has given the responsibility to 'have dominion over the fish of the sea, and over the birds of the air, and over the cattle, and over all the wild animals of the earth, and over every creeping thing that creeps upon the earth' (Gen. 1.26). Discipleship is about making that petition, 'your kingdom come', as real as our desire to hallow God's name and to do his will. We are not expected to do everything – but the challenges that face us each day are enough to be getting on with. Discipleship and the Coming Kingdom are therefore intertwined, as the following Advent intercession makes clear:

In joyful expectation of his coming to reign,
we pray to Jesus.

Come to your Church as Lord and Judge.
We pray for . . .

Help us to live in the light of your coming
and give us a longing for your Kingdom.
Maranatha.
Amen. Come, Lord Jesus.

Come to your world as King of the nations.
We pray for . . .
Before you rulers will stand in silence.
Maranatha.
Amen. Come, Lord Jesus.

Come to the suffering as Saviour and comforter.
We pray for . . .
Break into our lives
where we struggle with sickness and distress,
and set us free to serve you for ever.
Maranatha.
Amen. Come, Lord Jesus.

Come to us as shepherd and guardian of our souls.
We remember . . .
Give us with all the faithful departed
a share in your victory over evil and death.
Maranatha.
Amen. Come, Lord Jesus.

Come from heaven, Lord Jesus, with power and great
    glory.
Lift us up to meet you,
that with (N and) all your saints and angels
we may live and reign with you in your new creation.
Maranatha.
Amen. Come, Lord Jesus.[4]

Access leads us to discipleship, and they both take us to the
question of *inclusion* and *exclusion*, that image of the prison
house, from which we are to be freed. History is full of ex-

amples both of self-limitation, like the trend discernible from
the fourth century onwards of people not to come forward for
communion, because they felt unworthy, to the practice of 'ex-
communication', found in both the Roman Catholic Church
and in the more conservative forms of Protestantism. In our
own day, the Eucharist is probably being celebrated with
greater frequency than ever before, and there are some places
where, it would seem, the only qualification for receiving communion is to be able to open one's mouth. Moreover, the contemporary desire to include people in as much as possible, and
not to cause offence to them, is understandably strong, and
raises questions about the need for strong liturgies of the Word
with their own symbolic actions when that is appropriate.
Some Anglicans are so sensitive about the possible presence of
a considerable number of non-communicants that they refrain
from celebrating the Eucharist when a new priest is installed
in a parish. Yet there are occasions when the Church should
not deny herself this heavenly food, just because there may be
some for whom it is too much to step forward, either because
of personal integrity, or (sadly) because of the disciplines of
their own church.

There is the burning question, too, about admitting to
communion before confirmation, which I suspect is going to
carry on indefinitely into the future, as church life fragments
even more. It can become impossible to differentiate between
the spiritual awareness of a growing child and an adult for
whom a few religious habits gained a long time ago don't seem
to have done a great deal of lasting good.[5] Perhaps George
Herbert, that wise seventeenth-century parish priest and poet,
puts things succinctly and appositely in his *Country Parson*:

> The Country Parson being to administer the sacraments, is
> at a stand with himself, how and what behaviour to assume
> for so holy things. Especially at Communion times he is in
> great confusion, as being not only to receive God, but to
> break and administer him. Neither finds he any issue in this,
> but to throw himself down at the throne of grace, saying,

'Lord, thou knowest what thou didst when thou appointedst
it to be done thus; therefore do thou fulfil what thou didst
appoint; for thou art not only the feast, but the way to it.'[6]

Like the examples quoted earlier, whether it is the quiet
early celebration, the big jamboree, the Greek experience, too
foreign to Western Christians for our own good, or the care-
ful Lutheran balance of Word and Sacrament, all questions of
inclusion and exclusion have to start with ourselves. Too much
protectiveness of the sacrament has its own risks, and may
conceal our own inner fears that we have never faced up to.
Equally, a desire to include at all costs may just as easily conceal a casual approach to the life of faith that we carry around
with ourselves, as if to say, 'It doesn't really matter.' There is
a paradox here that is about God as mysterious yet alongside
us, distant yet near, accessible yet beyond all time and space
– and ready to make us disciples, even though following Christ
properly is at the end of the day impossible.

❧

We have looked at access, discipleship, inclusion and exclusion, issues that are raised by the imagery of openness and
being liberated from prison. We can now look at the antiphon
from the point of view of its overall sources, for they are rich
and varied. There is indeed a twist in the opening words about
the 'Key of David', for it immediately goes on to describe it
as 'sceptre of the House of Israel'. How can a key also be a
sceptre? The answer lies in the blending of the Scripture that is
behind these antiphons. It is not a case of straight quotation,
but, in the best traditions of biblical allusion, the original text
provides inspiration for something new and different. Many of
the best hymns are made up of echoes of Scripture, and some
of the worst are composed from wooden, unimaginative quotation. To describe a key as a sceptre is to invest the notion of
the key, which is about access, discipleship and inclusion, with
the royal imagery of kingship. The key is the sceptre, because

the key is a way of understanding the nature of the redemption Christ brings. Perhaps some further explanation of the antiphon is appropriate at this point.

The two main sources for this antiphon are curious, and for different reasons. The 'Key of David' that gives the owner the power to include and exclude (Isa. 22.22) refers to an interesting historical incident. Shebna was major-domo of the royal palace. He was punished for building far too splendid a tomb for himself, and was replaced by Eliakim – who in turn had to lose his job because of nepotism (Isa. 22.24–25). The message of Isaiah is clear: powerful people who use their power irresponsibly will inevitably lose it. And in the royal palace, no one – apart from the king – was more powerful than the major-domo, with his control over access to the king himself. Whether or not this series of incidents would have been picked up by the first users of this antiphon is of secondary importance. What is important is that the image of the 'Key of David' takes us to the royal palace, and the weighty responsibility of being a point of access to the King of Kings and Lord of Lords. One little incident, dating from around 700 BC, provides the inspiration for a meditation on the Coming Lord over 1300 years later.

The other source is the reference to those in darkness and the shadow of death. This takes us to the end of the Benedictus (Luke 1.79), the Song of Zechariah when his mouth is opened at the birth of John the Baptist. He sings of his son's future, preparing the way of the Lord, guiding the people into the way of peace. There is a double sense of the appropriate about this source, which reappears in the next antiphon, 'O Morning Star' (see Ch. 5). On the one hand, it provides further evidence of the fact that these antiphons were sometimes used in connection with the Office of Lauds (Morning Prayer), before and after the Benedictus canticle, echoing it directly ('to shine on those who dwell in darkness and the shadow of death, and to guide our feet into the way of peace'). On the other hand, it takes us to one of the central Advent figures, John the Baptist, the one who is the Advent access-point to the Coming Christ, the very agent of bringing this light and guidance to the people. The 'Key of David' liberates the people from darkness and the shadow of death, a place of fear and deep gloom.

Thus we have two quite different points of origin, a power-hungry palace official abusing his position, by mishandling access to the king, and a temple priest, made dumb for his lack of faith in the face of a promise from Gabriel about the son his aged wife is about to conceive (Luke 1.19–20), but now able to speak of the wonders that this child will inaugurate. The highest palace official and a temple priest chosen to enter the sanctuary and offer incense (Luke 1.9) – even such figures as these can get things badly wrong. To have political or religious power and prestige does not necessarily guarantee that all will be well. To have an important position in church or state does not preclude the possibility of things going awry.

Of course, God can redeem our faults, stripping both Shebna and Eliakim in turn of their responsibilities, and making Zechariah temporarily dumb. There is judgement in the truth of Advent – which should make us walk warily. It is not all sweetness and light by any means. The royal palace, or whatever its contemporary equivalent, whether it is the council chamber or the manipulative or bullying e-mail, is no insurance policy against the weakness of human nature. And the temple, or whatever its contemporary equivalent, whether it is the bishop's palace, the General Synod, or the argumentative parish finance committee, is no insurance policy against the enduring dullness of the Church at its most mundane and faithless. For it is Christ who holds David's key, according to the letter to the church in Philadelphia (Rev. 3.7), quoting this very passage from Isaiah. Access, discipleship and inclusion in Christ himself are therefore not to be taken for granted, and are better seen during Advent in the context of Zechariah's own words, the 'Benedictus' canticle, recited each day at Morning Prayer:

Blessed be the Lord the God of Israel,
who has come to his people and set them free.

He has raised up for us a mighty Saviour,
born of the house of his servant David.

Through his holy prophets God promised of old
to save us from our enemies,
      from the hands of all that hate us,

To show mercy to our ancestors,
and to remember his holy covenant.

This was the oath God swore to our father Abraham:
to set us free from the hands of our enemies,

Free to worship him without fear,
holy and righteous in his sight
      all the days of our life.

And you, child, shall be called the prophet of the Most
  High,
for you will go before the Lord to prepare his way,

To give his people knowledge of salvation
by the forgiveness of all their sins.

In the tender compassion of our God
the dawn from on high shall break upon us,

To shine on those who dwell in darkness and the shadow
  of death,
and to guide our feet into the way of peace. (Luke 1.68–79)[7]

## Notes

1 Rowan Williams, *Why Study the Past? The Quest for the
Historical Church* (London: Darton, Longman & Todd, 2005), p. 93.

2 David E. Ford, *Self and Salvation: Being Transformed* (Cambridge Studies in Christian Thought) (Cambridge: Cambridge University Press, 1999), p. 140.

3 *Common Worship: Services and Prayers for the Church of England*, p. 301; *Common Worship: Times and Seasons*, p. 40.

4 *Common Worship: Times and Seasons*, p. 36.

5 See Colin Buchanan, *Taking the Long View: Three and a Half Decades of General Synod* (London: Church House Publishing, 2006), pp. 52–68.

6 George Herbert, *The Country Parson*, Ch. XXII, in F. E. Hutchinson (ed.), *The Works of George Herbert* (Oxford: Clarendon Press, 1941), pp. 257–8.

7 *Common Worship: Services and Prayers for the Church of England*, p. 34.

# 5

# Morning Star

*O Oriens*

*O Morning Star, splendour of light eternal and sun of righteousness:*
*Come and enlighten*
*those who dwell in darkness and the shadow of death.*

'The music of Advent is solemn, but it's positive and full of hope,' an organist once remarked to me. That observation took me back to my days at theological college, when seven of us were dragooned into the local cathedral and taught to sing the seven 'O' Antiphons to the old plainsong chant. It was quite an experience having to learn the chant properly, and modulate the sharp rises and falls in music that has been sung in that way for centuries. The Advent carol service was based on these antiphons, and each was sung from a different part of the vast building, to maximize impact. The overall framework was a journey from darkness to light, the emphasis being on both sides of that particular spiritual coin. In the years since, Advent carol services have become very common, helped on by the provisions in new service-books, with imaginative sets of readings and prayer-texts.[1] Over and above this kind of framework, it is with the singing of Advent hymns, with their innate mixture of solemnity and hope, that most people identify, whether Philip Doddridge's 'Hark! The glad sound, the Saviour comes', written in 1735, John Milton's 'The Lord will come and not be slow', written in 1673, or 'Hark! A thrilling voice is sounding', a translation of an old Latin hymn probably dating from the tenth century.

The irony is that the first two of these hymns were not written for Advent at all. Doddridge was a Free Churchman, and in those days English Nonconformity knew no liturgical year. Milton was a Puritan, and the hymn was originally written as a poem. Shifts of this kind abound in matters of worship. Rather as in furnishing a house, new uses are given to older items, and they often fit their new surroundings better than the original context. The same process we have noted in the sources for these antiphons. They are echoes of Scripture, but the unity that results indicates just how well the various images, and the concluding 'Come' invocation blend together, with the same solemnity and hope that is suggested by the Advent hymns and music. The Coming God enters the darkness of the world – and keeps coming back for more.

The 'Morning Star' antiphon is about hope – and it, too, is a mixture of solemnity and hope. I remember that Advent service for the particular moment when this particular antiphon was sung – from the east end of the cathedral, underlining the image of the 'sun of righteousness'. That image, which lies at the heart of this antiphon, comes from the end of Malachi, the last book of the Old Testament (it probably dates from the fifth century before Christ): 'for you who revere my name the sun of righteousness shall rise, with healing in its wings' (Mal. 4.2). The background to this image is the sun-disk, which was very familiar in the Ancient Near East. Applied to the deity, the eternal light and life that it brings is healing for the nations, health and wholeness. It should come as no surprise that the same image is taken over to refer to Christ, the bright morning star (Rev. 22.16), who will come and 'enlighten' those in darkness and the shadow of death (Luke 1.79), once more. From the point of view of sources, it is interesting to note this second, sequential use of the end of the 'Benedictus' canticle, another indication that these antiphons were sometimes originally used at Lauds (Morning Prayer) as well as Vespers (Evening Prayer). Whereas in the previous antiphon the 'Key of David' provides liberation for those locked in darkness, here they are enlightened by the Morning Star of hope.

Like everything else, it is not the individual parts that are significant, but the sum of them all. Nevertheless, we who are apt to look at Scripture through modern eyes, and are sometimes less imaginative than we should be in handling it, need to develop wider perspectives, and realize that the Bible has been interpreted for nearly two thousand years. There is a long tradition of biblical interpretation – not least in passages like these, which proclaim the Christian hope as a fundamental attitude, cornerstone, and eternal truth to our faith. Here, for example, is what Theodoret of Cyr, in fifth-century Syria, has to say about the 'sun of righteousness', in his Commentary on Malachi:

> This applies to the first coming of our Saviour and the second: in the first he rose like a kind of sun for us who were seated in darkness and shadow, freed from sin, gave us a share in righteousness, covered us with spiritual gifts like wings, and provided healing for our souls. In the second coming for those worn out in the present life he will appear either in accord with their will or against it, and as a just judge he will judge justly and provide the promised good things. Just as the material sun in its rising awakens to work those in the grip of sleep, so in his coming he raises up those in the grip of the long sleep of death. [2]

Theodoret thus soaks this image with Christ, spurred on no doubt by his reading of the appearance of the 'bright morning star' right at the end of the New Testament (Rev. 22.16). In his Commentary on Revelation, Andrew, Bishop of Caesarea, in what is now central Turkey, in the sixth century, has this to say:

> He is the 'morning star', since he rose for us early in the morning after the three days. Moreover, after the night of the present life he will manifest himself to the saints in the

early morning of the common resurrection and bring to pass the unending day.[3]

And when we come to God entering the darkness of the world (Luke 1.79), this is what Bede, writing in a sermon in the first part of the eighth century, has to say:

Do you want to hear about the condition in which He found this people and what He made of them? The end of this canticle clearly makes this evident by saying 'the day shall dawn upon us from on high to give light to those who sit in darkness and in the shadow of death, to guide our feet into the way of peace'. He found us sitting in darkness and in the shadow of death, weighed down by the ancient blindness of sins and ignorance, overcome by the deception and the errors of the ancient enemy. He is rightly called death and a lie, just as on the contrary Our Lord brought us the true light of recognition of himself and, having taken away the darkness of errors, opened up for us a sure way to heaven. He guided our works so that we may be able to pursue the way of truth that he showed us and enter into the dwelling of everlasting peace, which he promised us.[4]

All three of these commentators have something important to say. Theodoret brings the two 'Comings' of Christ into Malachi's image of the 'sun of righteousness'. Andrew of Caesarea captures the Christian's 'reading' of the very end of the New Testament with its promise of hope and judgement by the Coming Christ. And Bede, the great Northumbrian, consistently ignored by biblical scholars and preachers alike, and yet one of the most original and influential writers of his time, hits the nail on the head when he works away at the image of God entering our darkness through Christ, guiding us through the errors of this world, so that we may 'enter into the dwelling of everlasting peace'.

Once again, we see how the sum of individual parts amounts to far more when we experience whole how the antiphon is intended to come across. Christ is invoked as the morning star, bringing light and healing to the darkness of this world. This is the Advent message, for it takes seriously what we are apt to describe somewhat naively as 'human experience', and is prepared to take equally seriously the God of surprises, the God of the future, the God of hope.

⌖

But how do we apply this message of hope? When I read passages like this, I want to have a way of making them my own, otherwise the Advent message goes over my head. How can I 'watch and wait' for this morning star, splendid in eternal light as the sun of righteousness, to come and enlighten me in my darkness, let alone anyone else? The answer lies in looking at our own experience in the light of our faith, and doing so in specific ways. Three spring to mind. The first is about the contrast between anticipation and judgement, which Theodoret explores. The second relates to how hope can become a reality where everything seems hopeless, which is what Andrew of Caesarea is encouraging us to do. And the third is about holding together images of the end of the world with our determination to carry on, with the divine strength that Bede so obviously believes in.

Anticipation is an inbuilt feature of Advent because of the rush to get to Bethlehem. This can take the form of those 'anticipatory' carol services, for which the Advent services are probably too sophisticated a substitute. The desire to get quickly to Bethlehem can seem irresistible at times. The Advent wreath is lit, one candle at a time – but that does not seem to be enough, because its subtlety becomes compromised by those who have an itch to improve upon its noble simplicity. Instead of consisting of four simple red candles, a fifth (white) candle is added, for Christmas Day, in order to resolve its ambiguity. And for good measure, one of the candles is sometimes rose-pink, to echo the 'rejoice' theme of the third Sunday, with its rose-pink vestments. This is a fairly recent development, if one takes the long view, and one which confuses rather than clarifies, and makes Advent look even more like Lent, because of rose-pink's once corresponding association with Lent's fourth Sunday. Christmas presents get opened before the Day itself, and some of us enjoy those Advent calendars, with a door for each day in December, until at last we come to 25 December, and all is revealed.

I wonder if there is something deeper going on in all this anticipation, which is about trying to dispel the mystery, trying to open everything up, trying to resolve ambiguity, trying to sort everything out in advance. It is as if we are incapable of that watching and waiting that is a vital ingredient of Advent patience. If you have never had to spend a good deal of time waiting in hospital for an important result to be revealed, then you have not yet experienced a particular sense of deep frustration at the personal level with the weakness of humanity, our humanity. A sense of uselessness pervades the human spirit on occasions such as these. All that is left to do is anticipate what one wants to hear and know. And sometimes there is joy, whereas on other occasions there is disappointment. Joy gives way to delight and relief. Disappointment engenders fear and anger.

Advent meets those very human situations head-on, precisely because it does not present life as easy, with everything sorted out, every anomaly resolved, every doubt answered clearly with certainty. The impatience that the patience of Advent requires of us takes us more and more into the heart of our faith. It fills us with a profound acceptance of our own limitations. Writing to his friend, Eberhard Bethge, in June 1944, following his arrest by the Nazi authorities, Dietrich Bonhoeffer sharply observes the difference between Christianity and a vague complicity with religious mythology in the relationship between this world and the next:

> The decisive factor is said to be that in Christianity the hope of resurrection is proclaimed, and that means the emergence of a genuine religion of redemption, the main emphasis now

being on the far side of the boundary drawn by death. But it seems to me that this is just where the mistake and the danger lie. Redemption now means redemption from cares, distress, fears, and longings, from sin and death, in a better world beyond the grave. But is this really the essential character of the proclamation of Christ in the gospels and by Paul? I should say that it is not.

The difference between the Christian hope of resurrection and the mythological hope is that the former sends a man back to his life on earth in a wholly new way which is even more sharply defined than it is in the Old Testament. The Christian, unlike the devotees of the redemption myths, has no last line of escape available from earthly tasks and difficulties into the eternal, but, like Christ himself ('My God, my God, why hast thou forsaken me?'), he must drink the earthly cup to the dregs, and only in his doing so is the crucified and risen Lord with him, and he crucified and risen with him. This world must not be prematurely written off; in this the Old and the New Testaments are at one. Redemption myths arise from human boundary experiences, but Christ takes hold of a man at the centre of his life.[5]

Bonhoeffer puts his finger on the essential unity between this world and the hereafter – which always brings us back to the unsatisfactorinesses of what we experience now: the waiting, the feeling of uselessness, the itching desire to achieve something, all those targets and strategies that so often fall flat. Dreams and visions matter, and they matter a great deal. That is why the Kingdom of heaven Christ came to inaugurate, and continues to inaugurate in the smallest and most insignificant events through our very smallness and insignificance, is a Kingdom not of this world, and not to be judged by human standards.

There is, however, another side to the importance of anticipation, of putting up with the world around us while still being aware of its eternal dimension. And that relates to the essential fragility of all that surrounds us. The tsunami of 2004 shook the world, and even now, there are calls for better use of the huge amounts of money raised, as if we were saying, 'Well, we can't manage the planet any more' (as if we ever could!), 'but we should still be able to manage our money properly.' Those scenes of vast waves of sea-water relentlessly pounding those shores will continue to haunt the survivors and their kin for many years to come. Disasters such as this, and others like them, may well be 'signs' of more to come, of climate change, of global warming, and much else. But they still hit us when we are off guard, and remind us that at the end of the day we are not 100 per cent in control of either our lives or our planet.

What Bonhoeffer does is to draw a contrast between the Christian faith and the mythological, which may be colourful in its own way, but will only touch us at the boundaries, not in the centre, to use his own words. Christopher Booker has recently analysed seven ways in which stories have been written down the ages and across many cultures: the first theme is defeating the beast, and he draws in such contrasting sources as the Anglo-Saxon myth of Beowulf and the American film *Jaws* – both of which are about a sea-creature that terrifies a local community until it is finally destroyed.[6] Doubtless we shall continue to need these myths, and re-tell them as well as turn them inside out (as we appear to have done in more recent centuries). They will persist in providing ways of living through experiences vicariously with the hero, and holding our breath while disaster nearly happens, or weeping when it really does. Booker's analysis relates to significant parts of the Bible, from Job to Revelation, with their colourful ways of describing how men and women of faith have struggled to make sense of their lives. But once again, they recall us to our fragility, and to that destabilizing sense that we are not over-lords either of ourselves or of the world and the environment in which we are set. The journey of faith, therefore, is not about a static, slick, packaged rule-book, with certainties on every side. The Christian hope can only exist in our environment as it really is – and not in some world of our own imagining that is far from real.

I used to yawn, mentally, through those bloodthirsty passages in the Gospels where Jesus describes in lurid terms the
signs of the end of it all (Matt. 24.1–14; Mark 13. 1–8; Luke
21.5–19), read in turn on Sundays before Advent starts. But
now I hear those words differently, especially when I note
Matthew's preoccupation with exclusivity, Mark's accent on
divine punishment, and Luke's deliberate placing of Jesus
*inside* the temple (when Matthew and Mark have him outside).
These variations help me to see more clearly that the earth is
as fragile as I am. And the sooner we all face up to these truths
– and do something about it – the better. Matthew's Gospel
(uniquely) follows Jesus' predictions with two parables that
are pointers to our responsibility in the life of faith. The first
is about faithful watching and waiting (the ten bridesmaids,
Matt. 25.1–13). The second is about faithful use of what God
has given us (the talents, Matt. 25.14–30). All three of these
passages are read in Year A in sequence, and they are their
own reminder of just where we stand with God: a fragile earth
that will one day pass away; the opportunity to watch and
wait, and be ready; and the proper use of the gifts we have
been given, different in each, since we may be equal in the sight
of God, but we are assuredly not the same. Anticipation and
judgement go hand in hand.

The second area concerns hope where everything seems lost.
This is where the old myths and modern stories can go no
further than describe and lament, because they do not have
the resources to do otherwise. They are nonetheless important, because they are the stuff of everyday life, many of them
are familiar means of communication in the secular world,
and the Bible relies on them as the background for many of
its narratives – not least in the passion of Christ, who can be
interpreted as the tragic hero.

This brings us to the tragedies of this world, which are under-
scored by some of the Advent music that sings of God entering

a sinful and dark world. Advent carol services often reflect this atmosphere, with candles in the dark (always a draw for a congregation). That experience answers the fifteenth-century English carol, 'Adam lay ybounden', which is known to many a choir in one or other of the twentieth-century settings.[7] Those words accurately describe the Advent hope – recognizing the intractable character of human sin, as well as the gift of redemption promised us in Christ. One particular context cries out to us – the apparent weakness and fragility of the Church.

It is a real scandal that disunity is accepted, even when we can work together far more than we do. At the local level I have watched congregations that are quite small gaining confidence by looking at themselves and their local settings, and discovering fresh impetus to become more faithful disciples, often in company with other Christian communities. We are not in the business of trying to be a commercial success, desperate to attract the attention of the world. What we are trying to do is find ways of being the church where God has placed us. One parish in the diocese found (to its surprise) an unusually high proportion of unmarried mothers in its midst – of which the congregation was largely unaware. A project to work with them and provide some help for them – a small beginning, but a real one – made for a local transformation of attitude. Similarly, another congregation discovered a new way of relating to parents and children after school, opening up a new potential for mission that made the important bridge between the conventional building, intimidating and unfamiliar for many people, and the church as the people of God at the school. In another community, a trainee police officer decided to get into the local community through the churches, their clergy and lay officials. Such bridges can be transformative. And they give the lie to the fact that everyone 'out there' (an expression used by many an organization, not just the Church) is automatically hostile to Christianity.

It may well be that we are going to continue to be fairly unimpressive on the ground, as we have been for much of our history. But the measuring-stick for our ministry of hope must be fidelity to the gospel. The solemn but hopeful music of Advent points not to ourselves, but beyond us – to God. If there is one lesson that the contemporary Church is having to learn, that is to make do with less, allow a little to go a long way, and love ourselves a bit more than we do. It is not the times that are troublesome – but the human race. That is how things have always been. Such an observation does not in any way diminish the real possibility of change – hence Advent's constant, disquieting message of hope.

⋅⁘⋅

This brings us, third, to the wider need to keep going, when all around us seems negative, hostile and grim. The Church's problems of evangelism and mission look simple when we consider the wider world, especially when religion itself has played just a little part in producing historic hatred, whether in Northern Ireland or the Middle East. We can chide past mistakes, such as methods of colonialism in Ireland as a whole. And we can chide international politics – there can be little doubt that American and British foreign policy has contributed to the plight of the Christian minorities all over the Middle East, over and above any questions that we may have about military interventions there. At a practical level, however, John Gladwin writes movingly about a method of approaching these problems that is locally based, and starts by taking the local seriously, both in Ireland and the Middle East.[8] There is no Christian virtue called giving up on a situation, even if it means 'hanging in there', and doing little else. One example from history brings us into the orbit of a classic in the world of Christian literature.

In 410, the Goths sacked Rome. It was the beginning of the end of the Roman Empire, and it had a profound effect on Western Europe. Many, many people were amazed and shocked that such an event could happen at all. The invincible power had finally been checked, and checked hard. As so often is the case when this kind of catastrophe happens, there was a refugee crisis, and Augustine's North Africa played its fair share in hosting many of these people. Questions came to be asked by the Christian community about whether such things could really happen. Did this not spell the end of civilization? To answer these and other questions, Augustine sat down and planned a major book, entitled *On the City of God*, which he began in 413 and completed in 427, by which time the invaders were reaching Augustine's own area. It is a monumental work, in which he takes on the paganism of his time, the superficiality of its culture, and the central part Christianity had to play in the future.

Contrasting the two 'Cities', the earthly and the heavenly, he identified three options over how to respond to what had happened. Either go with the flow, and give up on the situation, which would be a tempting proposition since (it could be argued) it is not really my problem. Or retreat into a ghetto of the likeminded, a comfort zone of the religious, where we can talk to each other in language that we all understand, and shut out the world at all costs. Neither of these courses of action will do for Augustine. Instead, he holds out a third – and far braver and more complex – alternative. He advises his readers to keep going, in faithful discipleship and witness, however difficult the going is, never giving up in the belief that God is at work in redeeming at least some of what is going on. Towards the end of this work, he articulates the Christian hope in terms that hardly come from an ivory tower: 'The supreme good of the city of God is perfect and eternal peace, not such as mortals pass into and out of by birth and death, but the peace of freedom from all evil.' And he goes on to apply these truths to the present life:

> The true blessings of the soul are not now enjoyed; for that is not true wisdom which does not direct its prudent observations, resolute performance, virtuous self-restraint, and just arrangements of these things, to that end in which God will be all in all in a secure eternity and perfect peace.[9]

86

Augustine's vision is fed on a passionate faith in God, a God he came to know and love after trying the other religious and philosophical alternatives on offer in the conceptual market-place of his time. His advice about not giving in to the prevailing culture, nor retreating into a separate, religious existence, but keeping going in spite of the often harsh world we live in is just as apposite today as it was then. In a similar vein, Maria Boulding brings us back to the question of whether there is a God behind and beyond all that we see and do, the fragile earth that could be blown apart at any moment by our own stupidity, or which we may wear out through our own folly and greed:

> If there is a Creator who stands outside the whole cosmic evolutionary process, and yet works his will within it by a wisdom and love that are present in its every tiniest move-ment, then human life has a purpose. It begins from God, and is on its way to a goal which, however unimaginable, will give meaning to the whole adventure.[10]

Hope that is deeply Christian, therefore, takes this life serious-ly and does not try to escape from it. Among the many hymns and chants that make up the music of Advent is a seventeenth-century French responsory with a haunting plainsong melody, which blends together some of the finest sentiments of the central and latter parts of the Book of Isaiah. It is a journey through realism, penitence, divine strength – and, ultimately, hope:

> Pour down, O heavens, from above,
> and let the skies rain down righteousness.                Isa. 45.8

> Turn your fierce anger from us, O Lord,
> and remember not our sins for ever.
> Your holy cities have become a desert,

Zion a wilderness, Jerusalem a desolation;
our holy and beautiful house,
where our ancestors praised you.       Isa. 64.9a, 10, 11a


Pour down, O heavens, from above . . .


We have sinned, and become like one who is unclean;
we have all withered like a leaf,
and our iniquities like the wind have swept us away.
You have hidden your face from us,
and abandoned us to our iniquities.       Isa. 64.6, 7b


Pour down, O heavens, from above . . .


You are my witnesses, says the Lord,
and my servant whom I have chosen,
that you may know me and believe me.
I myself am the Lord, and none but I can deliver;
what my hand holds, none can snatch away.
                                    Isa. 43.10a, 11, 13b


Pour down, O heavens, from above . . .


Comfort my people, comfort them;
my salvation shall not be delayed.
I have swept your offences away like a cloud;
fear not, for I will save you.
I am the Lord your God, the Holy One of Israel,
your redeemer.       Isa. 40.1a, 46.13b, 44.22, 43.5, 3


Pour down, O heavens, from above . . .[11]


*Notes*

1 See *Common Worship: Times and Seasons*, pp. 44–9.
2 Theodoret of Cyr, Commentary on Malachi 4.2; quoted from Alberto Ferreiro (ed.), *Ancient Christian Commentary on Scripture: Old*

*Testament XIV: The Twelve Prophets* (Downers Grove: Inter-Varsity Press, 2003), p. 311.

3 Andrew of Caesarea, Commentary on the Apocalypse 22.16, quoted from William C. Weinrich (ed.), *Ancient Christian Commentary on Scripture: New Testament XII: Revelation* (Downers Grove: Inter-Varsity Press, 2005), p. 406.

4 Bede, Homilies on the Gospels, 2.20, quoted from Arthur A. Just Jr (ed.), *Ancient Christian Commentary on Scripture: New Testament III: Luke* (Downers Grove: Inter-Varsity Press, 2003), pp. 33–4.

5 Eberhard Bethge (ed.), *Dietrich Bonhoeffer: Letters and Papers from Prison* (London: SCM, 1971), pp. 336–7 (from a letter dated 21 June 1944).

6 Christopher Booker, *The Seven Basic Plots: Why We Tell Stories* (London/New York: Continuum, 2004).

7 See Malcolm Archer and Stephen Cleobury, *Advent for Choirs* (Oxford: Oxford University Press, 2000), p. 1 (by Philip Ledger); I am indebted to David Price, Organist of Portsmouth Cathedral, for much help here.

8 John Gladwin, *Love and Liberty: Faith and Unity in a Postmodern Age* (London: Darton, Longman & Todd, 1998), particularly Section II.

9 Augustine, *On the City of God*, 19.20; quoted (with adaptations) from *The Nicene and Post-Nicene Fathers* (First Series) (Vol. II) (Edinburgh: T. & T. Clark, 1993), p. 414; for an introduction to the *City of God*, see the article by Ernest L. Fortin, in Allan D. Fitzgerald, OSA (ed.), *Augustine Through the Ages: An Encyclopedia* (Grand Rapids: Eerdmans, 1999), pp. 196–201.

10 Maria Boulding, *The Coming of God* (Norwich: Canterbury Press, 2001), p. 146.

11 *Common Worship: Times and Seasons*, p. 60.

# 6

# King of the Nations

O Rex Gentium

*O King of the nations, and their desire,*
*the cornerstone making both one:*
*Come and save the human race, whom you fashioned from clay.*

To describe God as King is to give him, for the first and only time in these antiphons, a role that we can identify with, rather than a quality (like Wisdom) or a biblical symbol (like Key of David). But monarchy, as we know from the Old Testament itself, can be a mixed blessing, because there have been good kings (like David) and less good kings (like Ahab). Moreover, to use the analogy of kingship in relation to God may have the advantage of immediacy, something we can relate to our own history, especially if we live in a monarchy, but it has disadvantages as well. Kingdoms vary in size. Kings can be described in geographical terms, such as King of Great Britain and Northern Ireland, or in ethnic terms, such as King of the Belgians. Kings can rub up against each other in such a way as to destroy each other, as happened in central and eastern Europe after the First World War. Kings, too, can be known for their cruelty, like Ivan the Terrible in seventeenth-century Russia, just as they can be known for their shrewdness, like Elizabeth I in sixteenth-century England.

In a recent book about kingship and monarchy, the television interviewer Jeremy Paxman[1] belies his reputation as a fierce interlocutor on current affairs by producing what has turned out for many people to have been a remarkably positive assessment of the monarchy in the United Kingdom. Of course, he does not pull his punches when it comes to human weakness, whether it concerns some of the monarchs themselves or their families. Nor does he confine himself to one country, for his travels in history take him to Austria, and his travels into the human spirit delve deep into why it is that northern Europe has retained its monarchies, along with Spain, adapting this historic institution to the development of democracy.

Thus we have the Queen of Denmark delivering what is invariably a well-presented and well-received lecture every New Year on a given subject from her rich repertoire of knowledge and experience. In a small country, as with a bishop in a small diocese, such a 'conversation' is easier to expedite than on a much larger scale. Juan Carlos of Spain managed – some say by a whisker – to take his country into a new era, after the long years of dictatorship under General Franco. In a more multicultural country such as the United Kingdom, that kind of relationship would be far more difficult. The Queen 'converses' with the people through a relentless sequence of public appearances, in which she shows not just remarkable stamina but an insatiable interest in whomever she meets, and whatever she is supposed to be doing.

Questions are raised about the hereditary principle, already under severe pressure in an institution like the House of Lords. Why should someone get a particular job simply because he or she is born to it? Paxman wrestles with this question, realizing that the monarchy would appear to be the last such role left to which the occupant is born and not elected, or chosen in some other way. He goes through history, revealing exactly when monarchs emerged with dubious competitive claims, like Henry VII, or were got rid of by execution, like Charles I, or forced out, like Edward VIII. But even allowing for these exceptions, we are left with the hereditary principle, albeit ripe and ready for adaptation when things suddenly do not work out.

The heart of the matter, however, is reached when he has to face up to the relationship between the British monarchy and the churches, the sheer fact that, although a new monarch is proclaimed on the death of the predecessor, there still has to be a coronation. However much this has been changed and adapted down the centuries, including (as with Elizabeth II) finding a significant role for the Moderator of the General Assembly of the Church of Scotland, it remains a Christian act of worship, a Church of England Eucharist. However uneasy Paxman has to make himself out to be about this particular aspect of monarchy, he nonetheless ends up with an explanation of the enduring significance of the institution based on its mystique, its representative character, the way it binds monarch and people together. And he even suggests that when the monarch, or her children, get things slightly wrong, this is an implicit way by which they are held accountable to the people themselves. There is, therefore, a profound 'mutuality' in the monarch–people relationship.

These observations quickly become the kind of baggage that we bring to the analogy of kingship when applied to God. They reveal both the limitations and the possibilities of the use of the term in relation to God – whom we do not elect, yet may choose to believe in, or cast aside, or even hedge our bets, while perhaps still feeling that sense of mystique, distance, from those who try to worship him. Moreover, the analogy of kingship in this antiphon is applied not to the world, as a geographical area, but to 'the nations', implying a different kind of relationship, one that is about different peoples, tongues, cultures. To describe God as 'King of the nations' is to make a claim of universality that transcends the local tribes of northern Europe, or the elected presidential systems of Western-style democracies. (Interestingly, it is the 'presidential style' of leadership elsewhere that is one of the most powerful persuasives for Paxman that monarchy is a Good Thing.)

To call God 'King of the nations' is to lay claim to his universality, over and above my particularity, and this is a promise held out at the end of the New Testament (Rev. 15.4). God is larger than my local concerns, my religious back garden, my small parochial world. I am constantly struck by this truth at the Eucharist when I reach the 'Sanctus' in the eucharistic prayer: 'therefore with angels and archangels, and all the company of heaven'. Here we have an even bolder statement, which pushes the analogy of monarchy even further, from 'the nations' to heaven itself, thus claiming a universality about every celebration of the Lord's Supper. It is no longer just my local holy meal, but the food and drink of new and unending life in him. The 'King of the nations' is also 'high King of heaven' – where past, present and future meet.

❦

Our antiphon, therefore, addresses God in terms of an earthly role and, in one of the shortest in the series of seven, takes care to define that kingship. God draws together the nations and 'their desire', what they want, making them one. God is therefore about unity in diversity. And we then ask that he come and save the human race – not just current believers, or the elite who are paid-up members of the Church – admitting that they are made from clay. Four main biblical texts underline this antiphon.

The first is from Jeremiah: 'Who would not fear you, O King of the nations?' (Jer. 10.7), to which is appended an echo from Haggai, the 'desire of the nations' (Hag. 2.7). This comes from a prophecy that concerns the People of Israel in exile. They are not to learn the religious ways of the people among whom they are living. They should stick to the ways they have learned before. God is not a tribal god, to be worshipped according to whatever is local. He is 'God of the nations', not confined to one particular ethnic group. And here, as with the central part of Isaiah, we encounter Israel's growing awareness that they are not meant to be inward looking. Their faith is not about themselves alone. It is about everyone, hard as that may be for those who are wearied from the experience of being deported from their homeland, their temple, everything that is familiar.

The second text comes from the first part of Isaiah, which is full of specific prophecies, this one (Isa. 28.1–29) aimed at both the northern and the southern kingdoms, who are going to experience judgement by being overrun by the Assyrians. The southern kingdom (Ephraim, in Isaiah's terms) has made a 'covenant with death' (Isa. 28.15) – probably an alliance with Egypt, which will lead them nowhere. In order to counteract this folly, God is going to lay in Zion 'a foundation stone, a tested stone, a precious cornerstone, a sure foundation' (Isa. 28.16). Such a text is hardly likely to have been overlooked by early Christian writers, since it is quoted as a promise of Christ's role in the community of faith by the author of the first letter of Peter (1 Pet. 2.6), where the Church is depicted as a house of living stones.

The third source comes from a key passage in the letter to the Ephesians, where the work of Christ is described in terms of breaking down the dividing wall between Jew and Gentile (Eph. 2.14). This is part of a passage which figures as the epistle reading set for one of the Advent carol services, the vigil for prisoners and those who sit in darkness (Eph. 2.11–22).[2] Writing of this passage, Martin Kitchen accepts the view of some earlier biblical scholars that this 'wall' is a direct reference to 'the dividing fence between the Court of the Gentiles and the Court of Israel in the Temple', in other words, the part of the temple beyond which the Gentiles could go no further, a boundary of which every Gentile would have been aware. If Ephesians was written by someone later than Paul, but who knew Paul's teaching well (which is the view of many biblical scholars), then this is an endorsement of Paul's own teaching, that the cross had brought the Gentiles into the orbit of the gospel.[3]

The author of this antiphon seems to have imbibed much of the teaching of Ephesians, with the echo of making both one (Eph. 2.14), and Christ as the cornerstone (Eph. 2.20). This dividing wall thus becomes all the more important as an image of what the gospel has achieved in Christ. Divisions between people on grounds of ethnicity or religious background or culture become entirely secondary. Yet these are the very matters that we tend to put first: what does your passport look like? What God do you believe in (or not)? Are you ready and capable of being one of us? When the secondary questions take over and become of primary significance, the gospel is in dangerous hands. And it has been one of the sad struggles of Christianity down the ages to work away at these very questions, not always with conspicuous success.

The final source is that reference to the human race made from clay (Gen. 2.7). From the earliest times, Christian writers have wondered at the paradox of this statement, and it is therefore no surprise that this image should form the conclusion of this antiphon. The high God, the King of the nations, stoops to form us from clay, from mud, from dust. Such an act of creation recalls us to our origins, on the one hand at one with the kingdoms of this world, on the other hand at one with the kingdoms of grace (here and now) and glory (in the hereafter). To end the antiphon in this way is to end with a bump: the whole human race, not just the religious part of it, is part of the order created by God. Religion is not a strange hobby for those who like that sort of thing. To think seriously about where we have come from and for what we are destined is the privilege – and the need – of any serious-minded human being.

Once again, we are faced with a rich blending of different sources. Those time-honoured biblical images are drawn together to form a coherent whole: the King of the nations, the cornerstone, the dividing wall, and the fact that we are created from clay. There is a descending movement, from the highest and most universal, through the work of Christ, to the lowest and most particular – which is us. God's Kingship is unlike anything we can experience in this life. It is not hereditary: he does not hand over his job to someone else when the going gets tough. His Kingship is universal. To that Kingship we now need to turn, in some of the ways in which we can apply it to our Church and our world.

෴

The international scene has changed almost beyond recognition over the past 20 years. For many of us, the end of the

Cold War marked the start of something new, for which we had been longing. We began to look at history almost as if it were leading up to the end of the twentieth century as a new spring, the end of the conflicts that had brought catastrophe to Europe and much of Asia. But then things turned in an ugly direction. The suicide bombers who shook the world on what is referred to as 9/11 made the Western world feel very fragile all over again.

History began to be looked at in a different light. A recent example is Martin Goodman's study of the clash between the Roman Empire and Judaism[4] – which shows that the destruction of the Jewish temple in AD 70, so far from being 'inevitable' (until recently the fashionable way of describing great events), was in fact something of an accident. It began with conflict between Roman authorities and Jewish insurgents, but it continued in the temple precinct only as a result of soldiers acting in an undisciplined manner, and the Emperor Vespasian and his son Titus deciding that it was perhaps a good idea to finish it off while they were at it, even though that had not been part of their original plan. Even that catastrophe, it would seem, need not have happened. Yet it shook the world, just as 9/11 has done. It altered the parameters of the then known world, preventing, among other things, the Jewish temple being a place of pilgrimage, which could have been the case down to this day.

Nothing is necessarily inevitable. Ultimately, we are in the hands of God, the King of the nations, who formed us from clay, and has broken down every barrier that we put up in order to separate us from others, whether in the way we live, where we come from, or what we believe. These three distinctions are frequently confused in public discourse, but they are different. They have become slogans that elide into and out of each other: multicultural, multiracial, multifaith. I remember using them in that lazy manner and being taken to task: they mean very different things, and in any case, there is one human race, not several, which means that 'multiethnic' should be used instead of 'multiracial'.

The fact that they are used so frequently together betrays a deep anxiety about how we handle diversity, both in local communities and at the national level. This is as true of our political institutions as it is of our churches. I wonder at the fact that we have a Welsh Archbishop of Canterbury, a Pakistani Bishop of Rochester, a Ugandan Archbishop of York. The Church, it would seem, does not fare that badly in this area. But this is only scraping the surface. To put it more directly, multicultural means my being taken to a Chinese restaurant in Edinburgh as long ago as the 1950s as a special family treat after going to church; being confronted with a mainly Chinese clientele and listening to the folk talking in their own language, as well as my trying to handle chopsticks – this is all part of the multicultural game. At the simplest level, multiethnic means my being brought up proud of my Danish heritage, enjoying Danish food, observing Christmas in a Danish manner, and filling my house with Danish furniture. Multifaith means recognizing the different faiths that co-exist with each other – something the world has known for a very long time indeed – including that of the Jewish boy at my school who was excused the daily assembly, because (in those days) it was of a Christian character.

The United Kingdom is already multicultural, and has been for centuries. One only has to go to the shops in some of our towns and cities to realize this fact, to say nothing of where many of us go for our holidays abroad. It is all part of a world that has become smaller. And it rubs off on the Church, in the way that we use music from Taizé, just as we have been singing hymns from the middle ages and wearing vestments from the ancient world. We are also multiethnic, which means that we have Nigerian Anglicans in our midst, Filipino Roman Catholics, Korean Presbyterians, and American Baptists up and down the country. Many of those of other ethnic groups are not Christians – and only then do we arrive at the multifaith dimension.

Important as it so obviously is, the term still figures prominently in public debate, almost as a way for the secularists to get Christianity off the scene. Yet the fact is that in the most recent census (2001), 71.7 per cent of the population claimed to be Christian, and the next largest religious group, the Muslims, were 3.1 per cent, followed by the Hindus, 1.1 per cent, the Sikhs, 0.7 per cent, and the Jews, 0.5 per cent. Another census could well show some differences, but this is a very different picture from that which is often portrayed in some of our newspapers. The matter becomes yet more sensitive for many Christians, particularly for the Church of England, when (amid all the public rhetoric against church schools) we have pioneered multifaith Religious Education; and in the one Church of England school in downtown Portsmouth Muslim parents prefer their children to go there because of its religious character. On the ground, the churches are doing far more than sometimes seems to be the case in building understanding between different sections of our communities.

In the face of these different kinds of diversity, apart from recognizing their subtleties, what is the Christian to do, as we contemplate the truth of the 'King of the nations', who has broken down every single barrier, long after creating us all 'from clay'? The Advent question transcends culture (the Advent wreath comes from Lutheran Scandinavia); it transcends ethnicity (Swedes in London have popularized their S. Lucia procession); and it transcends the boundaries of faith (gathering people together from different faith groups, especially when there have been local incidents of one sort or another).

Dialogue costs, as does that local 'blending' which has always been the hallmark of strong communities, at ease with themselves, secure in their identities, whether these are primarily cultural, ethnic, or faith-based. Advent demands from us some clarity in relation to what these issues are about. Advent challenges the sloppy assumptions that these three issues are exactly the same – which they are not. It doesn't stop their being difficult, as the recent debate about faith schools in Parliament demonstrated. But it does require us to be rather more open with each other than we have been. The trouble with a 'multicultural policy' is that it can produce the very opposite results from what is intended, so that different groups (and their languages) are catered for so carefully that social cohesion begins to diminish. Creative and truly challenging multiculturalism demands of us a readiness to co-operate with local initiatives that will help towards a more tolerant and understanding society in the future, such as ensuring that our children cherish their own faith, while knowing more about other faith traditions than my generation managed. Advent is a season for the prophetic – for looking beyond existing boundaries and attitudes, and breaking down that wall of division that separates us from each other.

✽

There is, however, yet another dimension to the claim that God is 'King of the nations', and that is the issue of globalization. Economically, we are all interconnected. The United Kingdom's 'Big Four' – Tesco, Sainsbury, Morrison and Asda – seem to be moving towards something of a monopoly of the wider retail market. The Western and Asian economies are growing fast enough for there to be real concerns about the developing countries. In the face of these changes, the churches need to look far more at the ethics of management and economy than they have done. Peter Selby's prophetic book, *Grace and Mortgage*, argues for a far greater place for economics in the life of faith than many of us were aware of, even positioning it between the lines of Jesus' teaching about social and moral relationships. A typical passage is the following:

When it comes to the management of resources in society, we are heirs to an ancient and demanding wisdom. It comes from a world vastly different from our own, which we have been taught to consider primitive and many of whose privations we are mightily glad to have transcended. We have learned to attribute much of that improvement in our material standard of living to the ingenuity with which resources have been invested and human drive and ambition harnessed to create prosperity of a kind that our forebears could never have envisaged even in their wildest dreams.

And he goes on:

> It is not hard in such circumstances to turn our eyes away from those who are not – or, as we may try to hope, not yet – beneficiaries of such progress. And when our eyes are drawn to them we tend to see in them not so much an indictment of the means of progress we have used, or even a qualification of virtues we ascribe to these, but only a reason to double our stake and press on.[5]

In the face of these challenges, all our talk of God's supposed 'universality' is subsumed to the point of irrelevance under our own collusion with economic structures as they are. Thankfully, Fairtrade and other initiatives provide the means not just for token protest at some of the ethics of the multinationals but for collective action that makes a difference. And thankfully, too, these initiatives are increasingly shared by men and women beyond the usual boundaries of the community of faith, and who are certainly not easily labelled as the new-style ethical angry brigade of middle England. Globalization for the Christian should mean debt-cancellation, and a proper regard for the weak in relation to the strong. One of the great boons in the Anglican Communion is the proliferation of bilateral links between dioceses of one sort or another in the developed and the developing world. To take but one example, for some years now the Portsmouth diocese has been linked to Ghana, which has meant a constant flow of people, clergy, other ministers, laity, taking part in joint activities, from theological education to congregational development. People come back from Ghana with a proper experience of another culture – including services and sermons far longer than they are used to at home! – that puts much of our theorizing about multiculturalism in its place.

Globalization affects the churches' own structures as well, and here old differences keep resurfacing, whether it is in the Roman Catholic centralized magisterium, under the Pope, the much looser Lutheran World Federation, or the Reformed Alliance. The Anglican 'Communion', something that has grown as Anglicanism spread from the shores of Britain to colonies old and new, and beyond, really began to be conscious of the need for some kind of regular meeting of bishops when the first Lambeth Conference was convened in 1867. It arose out of a request from Canadian bishops who were concerned about the effects of liberalizing tendencies in theology at the time, and the view of Bishop John Colenso of Natal, who, among other things, refused to deny baptism to those who practised polygamy. Since then, a Lambeth Conference of bishops from all over the Anglican Communion has met roughly every ten years as a consultative (not a legislative) body, and it has assisted the Communion over a number of global controversies over the years, such as liturgical revision and the ordination of women.

More recently, the question of gay relationships has figured prominently (some would say too prominently) in intra-Anglican debate, resulting in increasing tension between the American Episcopal Church and the Anglican Province of Nigeria, following the election of an actively gay diocesan bishop in New Hampshire, USA. A Commission under the former Primate of All Ireland, Dr Robin Eames, produced the Windsor Report in 2004, which proposed an Anglican Covenant, which would serve as a means for holding the Communion together, and to which member provinces could somehow sign up or not, as the case may be.[6] This issue, and the strategy under discussion somehow to 'deal' with it speedily, is a symptom of a globalized Church existing in a globalized world, where the tensions between the global and the local have broken out in a way that has not happened quite like this before.[7]

The important words here are 'quite this way', for history is full of lessons from the past, where profound differences have been handled more constructively and diversity cherished. The way we nowadays write the history of worship, for example, takes far more seriously the Third World and Asia than it has done before, to say nothing of the Ancient Oriental churches. These are the very Christian communities that grew up far closer to the earliest forms of Christianity in the Ancient Near East than the multinationals such as the Greek Orthodox and the Roman Catholics, and which are now suffering under Islamic pressure even more than they have in the past.[8]

History can help us to learn from the past to value the local, and not repeat old mistakes, as when the Ancient Oriental Churches (Syrian Orthodox, Armenian, Coptic) found themselves forced out from 'Orthodoxy' for reasons that to us now seem more political, cultural and linguistic than real. It is extraordinary to find difference so controversial, as in the case of early baptismal practice. Here, for example, is Ambrose, Bishop of Milan in the latter half of the fourth century, having to defend the old Milanese custom of washing the feet of those who have just been baptized, for the simple reason that such a practice was unknown at Rome:

> We are aware that the Roman Church does not follow this custom, although we take her as our prototype, and follow her rite in everything. But she does not have this rite of the washing of the feet. Perhaps it is because of the large numbers that she has ceased to practise it. But there are those who try to excuse themselves by saying that it should not be performed as a mystery, not as part of the baptismal rite, not for regeneration, but that this washing of the feet should be done as a host would do it for his guests. However, humility is one thing, sanctification another.

And he concludes: 'I wish to follow the Roman Church in everything: but we too are not devoid of common sense. When a better custom is kept elsewhere, we are right to keep it here also.'[9]

It would be tempting to dismiss this scintillating passage as nothing more than an interesting sideline from the past. But it says a great deal about how the fourth-century Church was struggling with the question of diversity, and at a time when baptism was (still) a most important 'marker', a rite of passage that identified the candidates in a very public and dramatic manner. Ambrose has obviously been challenged about an old custom that he has decided to retain, one that clearly had a great deal of meaning for his community. He was not going to relegate the washing of the feet to another, subsidiary occasion. Diversity even (especially?) at an occasion like baptism had to be worked at, especially when it was identified as a potential problem. Things do not change much in the Christian community. Is it better to rush into schism, or to work at disagreements in order to discern where they are really located, and then try to live with them?

To invoke God as King of the nations, through Christ, who has broken down the walls of our divisions, for us, who were created from clay, is to invoke the God of forgiveness and mercy. Among the liturgical provisions for Advent is a series of penitential litanies for use at the Advent wreath. The one appointed for the Second Sunday seems particularly appropriate here:

Heavenly Father,
you call us to repent of our sins:
soften our proud and stubborn hearts.
Lord, have mercy.

Lord Jesus,
you declared the forgiveness of God:
teach us to forgive one another.
Christ, have mercy.

Holy Spirit,
you search our hearts and show us the truth:
direct us in your way of righteousness.
Lord, have mercy.

Almighty God,
who in Jesus Christ has given us
a kingdom that cannot be destroyed,
forgive you your sins,
open your eyes to God's truth,
strengthen you to do God's will,
and give you the joy of his kingdom,
through Jesus Christ our Lord.[10]

## Notes

1 Jeremy Paxman, *On Royalty* (London: Viking, 2006).

2 *Common Worship: Times and Seasons*, p. 47.

3 See Martin Kitchen, *Ephesians* (New Testament Readings) (London: Routledge, 1996), p. 65.

4 See Martin Goodman, *Rome and Jerusalem: The Clash of Ancient Civilisations* (London: Allen Lane, 2006).

5 Peter Selby, *Grace and Mortgage: The Language of Faith and the Debt of the World* (London: Darton, Longman & Todd, 1997), pp. 140–1.

6 *The Lambeth Commission on Communion: The Windsor Report* (London: Anglican Communion Office, 2004).

7 See John Gladwin, 'The Local and the Universal and the meaning of Anglicanism', a paper read to the Ecclesiastical Law Society, January 2007.

8 See, for example, Geoffrey Wainwright and Karen Westerfield Tucker (eds), *The Oxford History of Christian Worship* (Oxford: Oxford University Press, 2006).

9 Ambrose, *De Sacramentis* 3.5, in E. C. Whitaker, *Documents of the Baptismal Liturgy* (third edition edited by Maxwell E. Johnson) (Alcuin Club Collections 79) (London: SPCK, 2003), p. 180.

10 *Common Worship: Times and Seasons*, pp. 56–7.

# 7

# *Emmanuel*

## *O Emmanuel*

*O Emmanuel, our king and lawgiver,*
*the hope of all the nations and their Saviour:*
*Come and save us, O Lord our God.*

We now come to the seventh and final antiphon in the series. In many respects, it comes across as much as a summary of the sequence as a composition in its own right. But in any sequence there has to be a beginning and an ending, and by its brevity and succinctness it speaks of the Advent message of the Coming Lord. But it does read surprisingly differently from the others, since it is made up of seven titles in all: Emmanuel, king, lawgiver, hope, Saviour, Lord and God.[1] Such an assembly of titles is unique in the series, and when we look at them more closely, it is easy to see why.

'Emmanuel' echoes the main biblical source (Isa. 7.14), being the Hebrew word for 'God with us', which we shall be looking at later. 'God with us' is the Advent message that transcends all others. In spite of the difficulties of life as we know it, the consequences of human sin and wilfulness, God is still prepared to take us seriously, and be 'with us', not estranged from us, not retaliating at us because we refuse to walk in his ways. 'Emmanuel' is, above all, the title that best expresses the message as Advent points us towards the three prongs of the future – daily discipleship, the annual commemoration of the Nativity and the ultimate Coming of Christ at the end of time.

Each one of those three dimensions to the life of faith circumscribes our daily living, so that each day does not exist in some kind of isolation, but is part of a coherent whole, for all that things often appear to be otherwise. Daily, yearly, eternally – these are the dimensions of the Advent message. We pray in the Lord's Prayer, 'give us today our daily bread', locating ourselves in time, as we go on to pray for forgiveness for the past, and protection in the future, whether from temptation or evil. That second part of the prayer sets us in history and eternity.

Then we have three titles that refer directly back to preceding antiphons: king (King of the nations), lawgiver (Adonai), and hope (Morning Star). The Kingship of God refers to his Kingdom, which will last for ever, and which Christ comes both to proclaim and inaugurate. It is not just something that will happen one day. If we take the Gospels seriously ourselves, then how we live now matters, and bears some relation to the hereafter – even if the details of that relationship are only drip-fed to us in this life, and we never quite understand them entirely. 'Lawgiver' draws together the two great mountain experiences recounted in the Scriptures, Moses on Sinai (Ex. 24.12) and Jesus preaching what Augustine was first to call the 'Sermon on the Mount' (Matt. 5—7). The God we believe in does not over-legislate, creating new crimes by the day, and filling prisons to overflowing, but works through the more subtle approach of motivation and challenge, another feature of Jesus' own life and ministry. And lest we are tempted to fall back on the Old Testament alone (which Christians under pressure to speak and act quickly are not unknown to do), we have the Transfiguration narratives (Matt. 17.1–8; Mark 9.2–8; Luke 9.28–36), where both Moses and Elijah are seen to be in conversation with Christ, at the end of which the three disciples, Peter, James and John, see only Jesus.

The three remaining titles, Saviour, Lord and God, cannot be said to echo in any direct form the remaining antiphons, Wisdom, Root of Jesse, and Key of David, except insofar as God is frequently identified with wisdom, salvation comes through Jesus, son of David, born in Bethlehem, and the Lordship of God, already proclaimed in 'Adonai', speaks of his authority over history. But to push these comparisons any further would be to destroy the poetry of the antiphon. What we are dealing with here is an all-embracing description of God, drawing together the previous titles and the sentiments behind them, as well as using others inspired by both Old and New Testaments, in order to make clear that we are praying these words in order to claim our privilege of direct access to God in Christ. 'Lord our God' is the language of conclusion – as if the sequence of antiphons were now looking forward to the future, not just to Christmas Day, but beyond, into the daily future of faith, and the eternal future of God.

The series of seven antiphons, however, merits further attention. Early use of these texts, and others like them,[2] betrays a hinterland of variations on other themes, including the regular use of an eighth antiphon, 'O Virgin of Virgins', in honour of the Blessed Virgin Mary. These antiphons, and others like them no longer in use, were spread over the season of Advent, until they came to be grouped together in a sevenfold scheme. Such sevenfold schemes suited the medieval mind well. It was Augustine who built on the foundation of his two great North African predecessors, Tertullian and Cyprian, to an interpretation of the Lord's Prayer divided very definitely into seven petitions; this was in contrast to much of the Christian East, where the petitions about temptation and evil were seen to be one, thus making six petitions in all.[3] But he went further than that. In his discourse 'On the Sermon on the Mount', written in 394 while a new presbyter, immersing himself in the New Testament, he applied the seven petitions to the seven gifts of the Spirit (Isa. 11.2–3a) and to the seven beatitudes (Matt. 5.3–10), an interpretation subsequently taken up and adapted by later writers. In fact, the number seven rang so many bells with preachers and writers as the middle ages progressed that there were attempts to relate them to the seven deadly sins, the seven virtues, the seven words from the cross, the seven Gospel words of the Virgin Mary, and even the seven orders of the Church.

With all these ideas in circulation, it is no surprise that the seven antiphons should have their own special treatment. In the mid-fifteenth century, Magnus Unnonis, a priest of the Brigittine Order at Vadstena, Sweden, wrote up a scheme for King Christopher of Bavaria, in honour of his visit to Vadstena, which not only set the seven antiphons next to the seven deadly sins and the gifts of the Spirit, but brought in the seven central events of Christ's life: incarnation, nativity, passion, descent from the cross, resurrection, ascension, second coming.[4] It is hard to know whether the preoccupation with seven was responsible for limiting the antiphons to this number, or whether seven emerged naturally – perhaps the former. As a mechanism for teaching, it was a useful way of relating different aspects of the gospel to each other, however fanciful it may come across to modern readers. This is all of a piece with an approach to theology and spirituality that wants to see things whole, rather than cut up into separate compartments. In the case of our antiphons, the effect intended was to connect Advent with Christian living (the seven deadly sins), the struggle for a better life (the gifts of the Spirit, as expressed in the confirmation prayer), and the Liturgical Year (the central events in the life of Christ). And it doubtless enabled these antiphons to be seen as a herald of Christmas in a wider way altogether.

As the last of the sequence, 'Emmanuel' brings us to the brink of Christmas. We may not be able fully to identify with some of these sevenfold schemes, but what we can do is appreciate their inner motivation, which is to see the Christian life whole. This is also what that late medieval reredos in Århus Cathedral sought to achieve in the artistic terms of the time. Advent does not exist in isolation, but is part of a coherent whole, the life of Christ working in us now, and coming to fruition in the hereafter. *Common Worship* provides an Extended Preface suggested for use during the period of these antiphons (17 to 23 December), helping to draw together all the main themes of the final run-up to the festival of the Nativity:

It is indeed right and good to give you thanks and praise,
almighty God and everlasting Father,
through Jesus Christ your Son.
He is the one foretold by all the prophets,
whom the Virgin Mother bore with love beyond all telling.
John the Baptist was his herald
and made him known when at last he came.
In his love Christ fills us with joy
as we prepare to celebrate his birth,
so that when he comes again he may find us watching in
    prayer,
our hearts filled with wonder and praise.
And so, with angels and archangels,
and with all the company of heaven,
we proclaim your glory,
and join in their unending hymn of praise:
Holy, Holy, Holy Lord . . .[5]

༄ཉྩ

One of the central features of these antiphons is the way they
blend together different parts of Scripture and reflect the different ways in which Scripture can be interpreted. 'Emmanuel',
however, has only one main source, and that is the prophecy
about the young woman conceiving (Isa. 7.14). There are
other sources, but they are less significant, such as lawgiver
(Isa. 33.2) and the hope of the nations (the Latin text of Gen.
49.10). But the most significant (and best-known) is the prophecy about the birth of 'Emmanuel'.

This raises questions about interpretation. Modern scholar-
ship directs us, first, to the context of the original text, and
tries to find a local, contemporary person to whom this might
refer. The young woman could be Isaiah's wife. Or it could
be King Hezekiah's mother. Another alternative (more likely)
is that there is no one particular person in mind, because it
refers to any young pregnant woman, as a sign of hope for
the future of the human race. Clearly Isaiah is taken with the

title, 'God with us', for he uses it twice more in a short space of time (Isa. 8.8, 10). To complicate matters more, the original Hebrew means a 'young woman', and not necessarily a virgin. Although early Christian interpretation applied this text to the virgin birth (we shall shortly see two examples), the Hebrew original was not entirely unknown to at least some early Christian writers, including Jerome, one of the best biblical scholars of antiquity, who flourished from the latter part of the fourth century until the first part of the fifth, and from his base in Palestine (unusually) studied the Old Testament in Hebrew.

How are we supposed to 'read' this text? All that the antiphon actually uses is the term 'Emmanuel'. But the context in which it is sung is preparation for Christmas, which means that the Isaiah prophecy that is its inspiration surrounds it. At one level, that prophecy is about any young woman, as a sign of hope for the future. But at another level, the way this passage is used in the poetic context of Christian worship and devotion leads us to a particular young woman who is with child, the Blessed Virgin Mary. Here are two different but overlapping comments on this passage. The first is from Tertullian, a tough-minded North African, who died in the first half of the third century. This passage dates from his later years, when he had left the Catholic Church because it was too lax for him, in order to become a Montanist (a kind of extreme charismatic):

What is this sign? 'Behold, a virgin shall conceive and bear a son.' In fact, a virgin did conceive and gave birth to 'Emmanuel, God with us.' This is the new birth: a man born from God. God was born in the man, taking the flesh of the old race without the help of the old human seed. God took the flesh in order to reform the old human race with a new seed. In other words, he spiritually cleansed the old human race by removing its old stains.[6]

The second is from the pen of one of the greatest of the fourth-century Eastern theologians, Gregory of Nazianzus:

Humanity was blended with God, and he was one. The more powerful predominated in order that I might become god, just as he became human. Although he was already begotten, he was born of a woman, who was a virgin. Because his birth was from a woman, it was human. Because she was a virgin, it was divine. He had neither a human father nor a divine mother.[7]

Both these passages use the Isaiah prophecy in order to explain the meaning and process of the incarnation – God with us means God born as one of us, yet retaining his divinity. Tertullian emphasizes the purpose of Jesus becoming man, whereas Gregory draws attention to the mixing of the two natures – 'humanity blended with God'. Such sentiments as these lie behind the use of this Scripture passage in our antiphon. It is easy to see why Christian writers from the earliest times saw this 'prophecy', probably originally intended to refer generally to a future full of hope, as a foretelling of the miracle of Jesus' birth.

And that leads us to consider the place of the Virgin Mary in devotion and Christian belief. In some respects, this is a bit like walking across a theological minefield with one's eyes closed! Not to put too fine a point on it, the roots of the Reformation run so deep in the hearts of some Christians that they tend to think of the Virgin Mary as a kind of dead Roman Catholic. There has been so much misunderstanding, not helped by some devotional traditions from the past that seemed to place Mary in a higher position than she properly merits. Fortunately, a more balanced picture has taken over. Yes, certain feasts were jettisoned at the Reformation, like the Assumption on 15 August, but no, she does not disappear from the Liturgical Year, because she still figures in February with the Presentation of Christ in the Temple, as well as on 25 March with the Annunciation; and there are other occasions, too, like 8 September, her Nativity. Moreover, writers such as Donald Allchin have helped us to recover a forgotten memory of the great seventeenth-century tradition of Anglican writing, such as the works of Lancelot Andrewes, Jeremy Taylor, Herbert

Thorndike and Thomas Traherne, all of whom paid great attention to Mary, the God-bearer, the 'Theotokos', as she is described in the Councils of Ephesus (431) and Chalcedon (451), a term that had already been in use for some time.

A good example of this forgotten strand of seventeenth century devotion comes from a poem by Traherne himself:

> And first O Lord I praise and magnify thy Name
> For the Most Holy Virgin-Mother of God, who is the
>    Highest of thy Saints.
> The most Glorious of all thy Creatures.
> The most Perfect of all thy Works.
> The nearest unto Thee, in the Throne of God.
> Whom Thou didst please to make
> Daughter of the Eternal Father.
> Mother of the Eternal Son.
> Spouse of the Eternal Spirit.
> Tabernacle of the most Glorious Trinity.
> Mother of Jesus.
> Mother of the Messias.
> Mother of Him who was the Desire of all Nations.
> Mother of the Prince of Peace.
> Mother of the King of Heaven.
> Mother of our Creator.
> Mother and Virgin.
> Mirror of Humility and Obedience.
> Mirror of Wisdom and Devotion.
> Mirror of Modesty and Chastity.
> Mirror of Sweetness and Resignation.
> Mirror of Sanctity.
> Mirror of all virtues.[8]

Some may not be quite ready for the lushness of Traherne's imagery. But to describe Mary as 'God-bearer' is to point to the *realness* of the incarnation. That title came into common use when there were those who wanted to spiritualize Christ's human side to the point where it lacked any proper identification with the earthly realm. One of the ways to counteract these claims (but by no means the only one) was to look again at the role of Mary in the work of salvation. The best place for us to start is with the Annunciation Gospel (Luke 1.26–38), which is read on the Fourth Sunday of Advent in Year B.

It begins by locating the scene in a time and a place – the sixth month of Elizabeth's pregnancy, in Nazareth. Mary is already betrothed to Joseph. Gabriel appears, and there are three exchanges between them. First of all Gabriel greets her as highly favoured, and Mary is too troubled to respond – which is a sign of her modesty. Then Gabriel tells her not to be afraid because she will conceive and bear a son who will be called Jesus. Mary immediately asks 'How?' – which indicates a spirit of faithful enquiry. Gabriel replies that the Holy Spirit will come upon her, and quickly suggests that she should not be surprised, since her cousin Elizabeth in old age has conceived, according to the will of God. Mary then responds that she is in the Lord's hands – an indication this time of faithful trust.

What are we to make of this? When Mary is troubled, she says nothing, because of her modesty. When she is told what is to happen in the future, she asks how this is to be, in faithful enquiry. When she knows the 'what' and the 'how', she commits herself to the Lord, in faithful trust. Here is an example of faith – that is prepared to be reticent, that is prepared to enquire, and that is prepared to trust. By contrast, we often find it easier to be immodest when troubled, to be glibly unquestioning when enquiry is more appropriate, and then to be insufficiently trusting when the purposes of God begin slowly to break through. In Mary, in the communion of saints, we find examples of faith – and we are one with them, in prayer and praise, in our own weaknesses, inadequacies and sinfulness.

Perhaps the greatest catalyst in engendering a more balanced approach to devotion to Mary is the rise in interest in eastern iconography, where every icon that westerners would describe as 'Virgin and Child' is interpreted more holistically as depicting the incarnation. Mary always points to Christ, drawing us to him, always a vehicle for that process, and not the process itself. Mary has an honoured place as the exemplar of faith, as the one who brought Christ into the world. To give her a place on her own is to exaggerate her position beyond what is right and proper. To deny her a place altogether runs the risk of turning Jesus into an idea, a concept, instead of a human being, born on this earth.

We may not all be able to ask for her prayers, 'now and at the hour of our death', as the fourteenth-century Carthusian monks started doing. But we can still follow those Greek Christians who from the fifth century, the century of the 'God-bearer', used the first part of the 'Hail, Mary' prayer, and with the angel Gabriel greet her as 'full of grace', because the Lord is with her (Luke 1.28). Such an approach to Mary's place in the scheme of redemption may help us to unravel the past, and enable us to empathize with fellow Christians whose devotional practices may differ from our own.[9] These antiphons, after all, are accompaniments to the Magnificat, Mary's own song, the song of God's chosen one, the song of God's promise of redemption (Luke 1.46–58).

♥

Before we conclude, it is perhaps appropriate to look briefly at some of the issues raised by the liturgical provisions for Advent. One of the features of contemporary liturgical revision is that we have become much more accustomed to using seasonal material. The current provisions in *Common Worship* are far richer than many of us have known in the past. It is good that we have the opportunity of such a unifying factor at such an important time in the Church's Year. They can help, too, to bring an Advent flavour into the many carol services attended by secular organizations, schools and academic institutions through the month of December.

The pre-Advent season concentrates on the world to come, whereas Advent's focus is preparation for Christmas, with John the Baptist and the Virgin Mary taking over as the season moves on – though it is sometimes hard for preachers (and musicians) to rise to two Sundays for the Baptist figure (Advent 2 and 3). The pre-Advent season, well-constructed as it so manifestly is, nonetheless suffers from the disadvantage of starting the new year on Advent 1, so that the preceding Sundays use the end of the preceding year's lections – which do not always fit each other. For example, when Year A ends, giving way to Year B on the First Sunday of Advent, the image of the Lord coming 'like a thief in the night' is heard twice (1 Thess. 5.1–11 on the Second Sunday before, and 2 Pet. 3.8–15a on Advent 2). It would probably be better to start the new Liturgical Year around All Saints' Day, and make that the occasion for the change of gear. This would have the result of harmonizing the pre-Advent season with Advent itself, by using the same Gospel as the primal source for the Gospel readings.

The eucharistic material follows the same kind of scheme as for the rest of the year, with introductions at the start of the service, seasonal penitential litanies, intercessions, eucharistic prefaces, together with blessings and conclusions. Perhaps the liturgical colour-scheme could change, so that not only is red used in the pre-Advent season, but blue for Advent itself, following medieval precedent, and preventing Advent from being seen as some kind of mirror image of Lent. What is also needed now is more provision for non-eucharistic services, which at this time of year can be in great demand, together with a set of shorter 'extended prefaces' that do not try to say everything at once. And some prayers for domestic use would also be welcomed. The themed Advent carol services give us almost more than we can cope with, in their rich use of Scripture. It is interesting to observe that what we have now is material that has been specially written for Advent. In the past, quite a number of Advent hymns were not composed for this season at all, including the popular 'Lo! He comes with clouds descending', with its richly inspired biblical imagery, which Charles Wesley included in a set of hymns of an intercessory kind in 1758. Adaptation has given way to custom-building!

'Come and save', ends the Emmanuel antiphon. We have travelled through these remarkable poetic compositions, with their echoes and quotations from Scripture, built on an imaginative approach to their inner workings and imagery. The progression from Wisdom to Emmanuel has taken us through many of the ways we try to understand God, as well as many of the avenues of human experience that we often try to hide from ourselves. It is not the only way to 'read' Advent. But it builds on an ancient way of relating to the great truths of the Coming Lord, which in time solidified into what became an established pattern of prayer in the evening, when the darkness has fallen, and the community of faith is singing the Song of Mary, the Magnificat. These antiphons even suggest the Christological and Trinitarian aspects of the faith that are the background of the season's fuller meaning: 'Come and save us – through Christ, in the Spirit.'

There is a sense of helplessness about singing that song when it is topped and tailed by these antiphons. This holds true whether we are contemplating 'Wisdom', as opposed to data; the 'Lord' on the mountain-top, not the power-crazed politics of our own age; the 'Root of Jesse', which delves into our own capacity to cope with continuity and discontinuity, not the often fearful and fretful initial reaction to any change; the 'Key of David', which challenges our supposed exclusive rights on Jesus; the 'Morning Star' of hope for a better world; the King of the nations, who coaxes us to look outwards to the sometimes terrifyingly globalized world from the sometimes suffocatingly narrow interests of the Church. Finally, we reach 'Emmanuel', the God who is with us, whether we like it or not, often sitting somewhat uncomfortably with our own preoccupations and priorities, above all confronting us with a new way of looking at a faith that knows when to be reticent, how to be enquiring, and why to be trusting. All this – and more – is part of the riddle of Advent. Each one of these antiphons enables us to see something new and fresh not only about the being of God, but his working, his 'energies', as the Eastern Fathers would describe them.

That helplessness I had to discover for myself, for the first time in my life, when I underwent a bone-marrow transplant in hospital. Enclosed in a room from which I was only allowed to go when required for an X-ray (and then only under supervision, and with an oxygen mask over my face), I had to lie in bed and get used to being watched and overseen by several different groups of people, doctors, nurses, physiotherapists, dieticians, each of whom had a specific agenda in order to help bring me back to a more healthy and prolonged life. There was nothing I could do but become passive and obedient, doing exactly what I was told to do, even if it was having my blood-pressure regularly taken in the early hours of the morning, along with all the other patients on the ward. I even had to report how much I was eating and when – and much else besides. I had never before known what it was like to put my total trust in others. Hitherto it had always been me actively participating in at least a part of what I was living through.

Something of this strange passivity has been going through my mind as I have written these pages. I suppose I chose Advent because this season seemed to spell out to me the passivity of faith in the face of the Coming Lord, the One who comes in that tantalizing but interrelatedly threefold way of daily faith, the annual preparation for Bethlehem, and the end of all time. And that is another part of Advent's riddle. I can just about cope with the daily Coming, and I have got used to the annual rhythms of the year, different as each one is when the days arrive. But the end of all time? Instead, I have had to consider my own death as a reality for the first time in the past two years because of serious illness. Yet even that is too individual, too specific, too unrelated to the other people towards whom I am beckoned by those seven Advent antiphons. In their studied and compressed eloquence, they stand as a sevenfold challenge to the culture in which we live, where – in the West – we have become so affluent, yet underneath lies a ferment of unanswered questions, unresolved fears, unnecessary unhappinesses, a condition described by Oliver James as 'affluenza'.[10]

As I watch and wait upon the Lord, I know in my heart of hearts that that ferment is not where I really belong, because I belong somewhere else. I may not be ready for it when I do die. But I believe that, whatever sense I can make of the 'Four Last Things', death, judgement, heaven and hell, we are – somehow, by the grace of God – destined for another shore, and a greater light. In his book on the Transfiguration, Michael Ramsey writes of these truths in his usual perceptive manner:

> The hope of the beatific vision is crossed by the hope of the vindication of the divine design not only in us but in all things. And the hope of the resurrection of the body, when the body of our low estate is transformed into the body of Christ's glory, is the reminder of our kinship with the created world which the God of glory will redeem in a new world wherein the old is not lost but fulfilled.[11]

## Notes

1 See Th. J. Knoblach, 'The "O" Antiphons', in *Ephemerides Liturgicae* CVI (1992), pp. 188–9 (whole article, pp. 177–204).

2 See, for example, Egbert Ballhorn, 'Die O-Antiphonen: Israelgebet der Kirche', *Jahrbuch für Liturgik und Hymnologie* 37 (1998), pp. 9–34 (an interesting study of the Old Testament background to these antiphons); and L. Colliard, 'Les trois messes de Noël et les antiennes "O" de l'Avent selon le rit de Paris. Une confrontation avec le rit romain', in *Le Flambeau* 1 (1982), pp. 65–72 (chronicling Neo-Gallican (French) independence from Rome over their order and number). I am indebted to Harald Buchinger for drawing my attention to these articles.

3 See Kenneth W. Stevenson, *The Lord's Prayer: A Text in Tradition* (London: SCM/Minneapolis: Fortress Press, 2004), esp. pp. 77–84.

4 See Knoblach, 'The "O" Antiphons', pp. 196–7.

5 *Common Worship: Services and Prayers for the Church of England*, p. 301; *Common Worship: Times and Seasons*, p. 40.

6 Tertullian, *On the Flesh of Christ* 17, quoted from Steven A. McKinion (ed.), *Ancient Christian Commentary on Scripture: Old Testament X: Isaiah 1–39* (Downers Grove: Inter-Varsity Press, 2004), p. 61.

7 Gregory of Nazianzus, 'On the Son: Theological Oration' 3 (19) 19; quoted from McKinion, *Isaiah 1–39*, p. 62.

8 See A. M. Allchin, *The Joy of All Creation: An Anglican Meditation on the Place of Mary* (London: New City Press, 1993), pp. 117–18.

9 See, for example, *Mary: Grace and Hope in Christ* (Report of the Anglican–Roman Catholic International Commission) (London: Continuum, 2004).

10 See Oliver James, *Affluenza* (London: Vermillion, 2007), for a devastating critique of our values.

11 A. M. Ramsey, *The Glory of God and the Transfiguration of Christ* (London: Longman, 1949), p. 90.